IT'S NOT ALL ABOUT YOU

Young Adults Seeking Justice

Julie Richardson Brown
Courtney Richards
EDITORS

CHALICE®
PRESS

ST. LOUIS, MISSOURI

Bible quotations, unless otherwise noted, are from the *New Revised Standard Version Bible,* copyright 1989, Division of Christian Education of the National Council of the Churches of Christ in the United States of America. Used by permission. All rights reserved.

Scripture quotations marked (NIV) are taken from the HOLY BIBLE, NEW INTERNATIONAL VERSION®. NIV®. Copyright © 1973, 1978, 1984 by International Bible Society. Used by permission of Zondervan Publishing House. All rights reserved.

Cover art and design: Scribe, Inc.

www.chalicepress.com

10 9 8 7 6 5 4 3 2 1   12 13 14 15 16 17

PRINT: 9780827216471   EPUB: 9780827216488   EPDF: 9780827216495

**Cataloging in Publication Data from the
Library of Congress available upon request.**

Contents

OK, so here's the deal...   v

Introduction (or, "Why This Book Matters")   vi
    Julie Richardson Brown

PART 1: Send/Receive

1 Call   3
    Marc Istook

2 Reflections from East Africa   13
    Shelvis & Nancy Smith-Mather

3 A War on Two Fronts   24
    Joshua Dobbs

4 Legacy, Responsibility, and Faith   32
    Kendra Dunbar

PART 2: Let Me Get Back to You

5 Difference Makes a Difference   42
    Erika Roman Saint-Pierre

6 Camp Bani   52
    Joe Geoghegan and Chloe Grammer

7 Current City: _____   59
    Michael Wagner

8 And Let's Be Honest...   69
    Joshua E. Perry

9 The Day We Didn't Go to Church   78
    Amy Jonason

PART 3: Static Disconnect

10 Frontera   88
    Dan Millis

11 Coffee Can Change   99
    Jennifer Fischer

12 **Stealing Back the Future**   107
     Kristen Walling

13 **The Slow Examples of Lifetimes**   115
     Katherine Bell and Jill Delaney

Conclusion (or, "Now What?")   125
     Courtney Richards

Contributors   128

OK, so here's the deal…

If you're like us, you've had plenty of "WTF?" moments with church and you asked one question.

No, not *that* one. Okay, maybe *that* one. At first. But that quick, flip question led to another, more important question: Where's The Faith?

Faith in a God who can be present in both scripture and science. Faith that allows us to meet our neighbors on equal ground, no matter their ethnic, religious, or economic background. Faith that folks in their teens, twenties and thirties have something to contribute to the world, that they have big questions and big ideas about God, politics, sex, culture, the economy, justice, and what it means to be a human being.

We decided we wanted a series that brought as many young adult voices to the table as possible to talk in authentic, honest ways. These aren't slackers. They aren't overgrown adolescents. Instead of being talked about, or having questions posed about them, young adults are the ones framing the discussion, pushing the envelope, sharing their stories.

Discuss these stories amongst yourselves, or discuss them with us (series editors Brandon Gilvin and Christian Piatt) on Facebook on the WTF: Where's the Faith? page.

Read on.

Brandon and Christian

Introduction
(or, "Why This Book Matters")

"Hey there!" a familiar voice said, and I frantically began flipping through my mind's Rolodex, having not looked at the caller i.d. before punching the phone's answer button.

"Hi!" I replied, stalling for time, thankful as I could be when the voice identified itself: "Julie, it's Jonathan. How are you?"

He went on, "I just wondered if there was anyone at your church who needed help? Or anyone else you might know of who needs someone to help them clean up or move or whatever..." In the twenty-four hours before Jonathan's call, our city had been overwhelmed by an unexpected heavy rainstorm. Major roads were closed, downtown businesses and neighborhoods were flooded, cars were stalled or floating, and all over people were trying to figure out what to do next. The majority of the metro area had no electricity and I'd worried all morning about our congregation's elderly folks. A smile curved across my face and my heart sang at Jonathan's words. I knew he meant them sincerely, and that if I or anyone else needed him, he'd be there in an instant.

Jonathan is in his late twenties, single, and a walking definition of the urban hippie. He drinks only fairly traded organic coffee, shops locally, rides a bicycle everywhere he can, eats more vegetables and fruit than anything else, and loves to talk about books and ideas and how we could change the world if we'd only try. He does all of these things out of a deep conviction that the world is not as it should be. But on any given Sunday, you will not find Jonathan in a church pew. He won't go, doesn't see its ultimate relevance, and has become so jaded by judgment and exclusion on the Church's part that he has chosen to live out his convictions (read: his *faith*) by living a life that seeks to put others first.

That day the rains came, this church-avoiding hippie's call was the first—*the very first*—phone call I received asking if anyone needed help.

For every Jonathan, there is also (1) a young adult desperate for meaning and purpose and (2) a young adult raised and nurtured by the Church in such a positive way that he or she wants to spend his or her life living Jesus' call to feed the poor, tend the sick, and clothe the naked. These young men and women understand there is more to this life than our tendency to measure success and fulfillment by how soon we qualify for a mortgage or how much stuff we can accumulate by age thirty. They get that the world is much bigger than any of us realizes, and that we play such a small part in it all, so we'd better pay attention to the rest of it if we expect our grandchildren to have any kind of future.

Some would say that these young adults are the exceptions in a generation focused solely on themselves and their *stuff*. I argue that they are the uncelebrated and unacknowledged rule. This book is for them, about them, and a product of their willingness to prove that today's young adults are capable of doing one better than the generations that spawned them, able to see that our culture's obsession with status and things is only a mad race to find meaning in a world whose soul has a gaping God-shaped hole desperate to be filled. Whether Jonathan and his peers realize it or not, they are crafting a future built on community and truth, justice and mission, grace and connection. And we are sorely in need of such a future.

Not long ago, I had the great privilege of sitting down with Will Campbell—author, preacher, and civil rights activist. I told him I was working on a book about young adults and mission and the Church, and that I was struggling, because so often I see young adults walking away from the Church in mass droves.

A sly grin that was half-grimace broke across his face as he asked, "Can you blame them?"

I can't.

Too often, the Church has been a place of judgment and exclusion, and, in a postmodern globalized world where we are daily confronted with what it means to be in relationship with people of widely varying ethnic, socioeconomic, and religious backgrounds and where our very American children really should make learning at least Spanish a priority, it is crucial that we find a way to open those narthex doors wider and make a little more room in the pews for people we don't know, like, or understand. Jonathan and his peers get this, and, as a result, are usually the first to walk *out* the front doors of their local congregations and *into* the world, *longing for the kind of wholeness that comes when we realize that our call to care for one another is really our only chance at making the world all that God meant for it to be.*

The stories you will find in this book will inspire you and challenge you; bring you to tears and cause you to chuckle; make you question truths you've long held dear and introduce you to ways of thinking you might not have known before. These stories have been written by young adults scattered across the globe—young men and women cynical enough to ask questions, and faithful enough to want to do something; brave enough to challenge what they've been handed, and clear-eyed enough to know that it is, in fact, *not* all about them.

It is about all of us.

Julie Richardson Brown

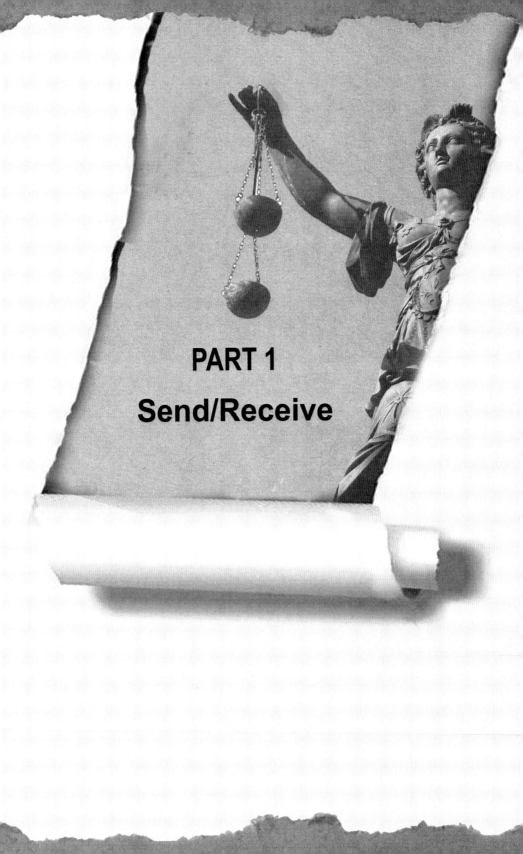

PART 1

Send/Receive

1

Call

MARC ISTOOK

Call.

Four letters. One word. Infinite meanings.

It's a word that speaks to the heart of our faith. Who does God call us to be? What does God call us to do? What are we called to believe? Figuring out these specific calls might be one of the most paradoxical aspects of being a Christian. Depending on who you ask, it can be simple or complex, easily discerned or never fully grasped.

One thing's for sure: *call* is definitely a buzzword in the Christian community. You'll hear sermons titled "Discerning Your Call," or "Listening for God's Call to You," or "God's Calling. Pick Up!" Ok, so I completely and totally made those sermon titles up, but I'm guessing that if an infinite number of preachers sat at an infinite number of typewriters, writing an infinite number of sermons, these are titles that would quickly emerge.

There are those who argue that our call is laid out simply in scripture. Others argue that God intends for us to wrestle with determining our call. And which God do we listen to? The Old Testament Father, who to many appears to be all about rules and accountability and conservative talking points? The New Testament Jesus, a Birkenstock-wearing socialist? Or the Holy Spirit, as determined by "What I Think God Is Saying to Me Today?"

Given that we can't always agree on what we're called to do collectively as a body, it's no surprise that it can be even more difficult figuring out what we're called to do individually. Making this all more difficult, when we sit down to determine our call, we bring all sorts of baggage to the table. Perspective, bias, experience, emotion, confusion, scripture, expectations, and more—all shoved into a suitcase.

Then there's the question of: How often should we seek a call? Am I called to take this specific job? Move to this specific city? Date this specific girl? Order this specific appetizer?

Given how tough and life-altering the process can be, sometimes I do wish we could just throw our hands in the air and ask God to make it a bit more clear for all of us. But where would be the fun in that? And then where would I seek inspiration for this essay?!

Obviously, different people use different methods to figure out how to answer these questions of call. For me, it's always been something of a hodgepodge: consisting of the messages I heard in church as a kid, the lessons my life experiences have taught me, scripture, conscience, and Oprah.

The conclusion these influences led me to is simple: *It's Not All About Me.* Incredibly convenient for the purposes of this essay.

However, perhaps the great irony here is that, despite the altruistic leaning of this collection's title, the focus of this essay kind of is...all about me. What I think. How I feel. The way I try to live in the world. Hopefully you can overlook the necessary narcissism here to see the bigger picture. I know I'll be doing that.

●

"He has shown you, O man, what is good.
* And what does the Lord require of you?*
To act justly and to love mercy
* and to walk humbly with your God."* — Micah 6:8 (NIV)

For some reason, this scripture has always been a personal favorite. And not just because it provides the lyrics for a beautiful camp song. To me, it lays out that concept of "call" in the simplest of terms.

What am I called to do? Well, God showed me. Act in accordance with justice. Love the ideal of mercy. Walk humbly with God. Period.

Oh, but if only it were that easy. What is just? And whose definition of justice are we using? How do I apply mercy in a given situation? And does that conflict with justice being served? Doesn't presuming my form of justice is wholly valid then negate the idea of humility? And can I come up with several more rhetorical questions to illustrate my point?!

Perhaps there's a dance here, between the simple and the complex. Obviously you can wrestle with nuance and the application of a message like the one in Micah. I'm certainly capable of that—tossing and turning over a directive, challenging it, trying to figure out "What It All Means," working my mind into a convoluted pretzel. But there are times when simplification is most valuable, when boiling a scripture, an idea, a call down to its essence is ideal. Maybe this is one of those times—especially given that we've got a 3000-word limit for this essay.

Simply put, I think Micah 6:8 (and, in my opinion, much of the rest of scripture) says, quite clearly, that It's Not All About You...or me. But it is about how you and I choose to live in this world. Justice demands that we elevate the rights of others, relative to our own. Mercy commands that we take another person's situation into account, his or her experience and obstacles and potential. Humility requires us to continually keep our wants and needs in perspective and to think of how they affect those around us.

So it's with those directives that I try to live my life. Simple? In theory, yes. In practice? I wish.

●

Justice is a "big" word. What it lacks in size, it makes up for in stature.

It represents concepts that provide essential foundations for our system of fairness and government. In its most common application, we use it in thinking about the justice system— how we treat criminals and adjudicate disputes. And that's absolutely appropriate. But on a more personal level, how does one live a "just" life?

Given that I'm not an attorney or a judge and have not yet served on a jury, I don't really have access to affecting the criminal form of justice. It's hard for the average person to "act justly" on that level. But bring up Glenn Beck's favorite term, "social justice," and my ears perk up. Now that's some justice I can sink my teeth into on a daily basis.

According to the Holy Grail of Internet Research, Wikipedia, social justice is defined as "…the idea of creating an egalitarian society or institution based on the principles of equality and solidarity, that understands and values human rights and that recognizes the dignity of every human being."

I like the sound of that. Reminds me of that Birkenstocked fellow and his take on things:

"Treat others as you'd like to be treated."

"The last shall be first and the first shall be last."

"As you have done it to the least of these, you've done it to me."

"Who's hungry and wants some free fish!?"

All kidding and massive oversimplification aside, the concept of finding ways to seek fairness and justice through social means rings true to me. It feels like the God I know. And it remains consistent with my Micah 6:8 affinity.

But again, how is this goal achieved?

I think the justice and humility component of Micah 6:8 tie together. If you see yourself as one of many people living in the world, you're more likely to consider how your actions impact others, whether that means economic decisions that directly affect another human being, or environmental decisions that seek to leave a hospitable planet for future generations.

So the first step is to become aware of what's going on in the world and to understand the impact of our decisions. It's easy to buy and sell and act, without giving a thought to what the consequences of those actions might be. But I believe that if you're not a part of the solution, then you're part of the problem. That compels me to consider how my actions affect others and to educate myself about the economic, social, and environmental situations surrounding those decisions. Is my desire for a cheap tomato causing some farm worker somewhere to toil in unsafe, underpaid conditions? Is my shopping at Wal-Mart contributing to that company strong-arming local municipalities into giving tax breaks that deny school districts the funds they need to educate children? Is the bottled water I buy dirtier, more expensive and worse for the environment than what comes out of my tap?

I'll be the first to admit that I've got plenty of work to do when it comes to being socially aware. I don't drive a hybrid. I don't research every company I patronize. I should do a better job in giving of my time and money to benefit those less fortunate than me. I should stop watching *The Bachelor*.

But I'm trying.

I'm trying to be the kind of Christian who votes with his pocketbook. Who supports political candidates and policies that benefit "the least of these". Who lives in a way that respects the earth and my share of it. Who improves the lives of the people I interact with and do business with (and the ones far down the line as well) in a way that represents the Christ I love and the call he's given me.

@Jenni *Perfection and an absolutely just life are not possible, but trying is essential.*

That, to me, is justice. And it's a justice we all have access to.

●

There are a lot of homeless people in Los Angeles—a whole lot.

They are downtown. They are at the beach. Sleeping in doorways. Standing in line at McDonald's.

The homeless issue (and, by extension, the issue of severe poverty) is a problem here that nobody has figured out how to solve. Of course, this isn't just L.A.'s problem. It's New York's. And Chicago's. And Europe's. And Africa's. In some form or another, it's the world's problem, really.

Of course, Jesus told us that the poor would always be with us. And some people tend to think that's a license to forget about them, or to marginalize them, or to look the other way.

I like to think that I'm a special kind of Christian who deserves a pat on the back because when a homeless person asks me for spare change, I always give it. Shirt off my back, right? It's certainly one way to demonstrate a love of mercy. Look how merciful I am! Except, if I'm being honest, I hate being asked. And I've even crossed the street before when I know there's a homeless guy down the block who's going to ask me for a buck. Then I'd be forced to interact with him, which would remind me of his plight and induce guilt, which might last a few minutes.

Who wants that?

I may say I love mercy, but I don't always do a very good job of showing it.

If I truly believe that *It's Not All About Me,* if I truly believe that loving mercy is so important, why do I find it so hard sometimes?

I won't pretend to know the right way to address the incredibly complex situation of homelessness. But I do know the wrong way. And it's a way I take far too often. What I want to do, what I'm called to do, is to remember that this "homeless person" is a human being—someone possessing dignity and deserving of respect. Should it matter if this person is living on the streets because of a drug addiction or some perceived laziness, as though that excuses me from my Christian responsibility? Would it make a difference if it were because of an untreated mental condition? And even if it did matter (which it doesn't), how would I know what this person's story was if I never took the moment to have an actual, genuine conversation?

Interacting with the homeless population in Los Angeles is perhaps the easiest and most common way to demonstrate a love of mercy. Here are people in genuine need of interaction with another human being that doesn't end with a look of disgust or silence. It might involve helping someone with a couple of bucks, or just offering to buy a cup of coffee, or simply having a real conversation.

This isn't a topic I discuss with many people. Maybe writing this is cathartic in some way. Hopefully putting it in writing, being honest with myself about my failings in this area, will remind me to be a better human being. Maybe it'll keep me from crossing the street and limiting my interaction to handing a guy a dollar bill before sprinting off. Maybe I'll remember this the next time a guy asks me for a little help. And maybe I'll start doing a better job of practicing the mercy I claim to love.

●

The idea of a "thin place" is a concept I was introduced to at church camp.

Basically, a thin place is a location where the division between yourself and God is thin. You feel God's presence there, rather than the thick, distant removal many of us feel in our daily lives. A thin place can be a place in time, or a geographical location.

Ethiopia is one of my thin places.

Mission trips are funny things. In 2008, I was on a two-week mission trip to Addis Ababa, supposedly teaching English and culture to teens at a church there. But the truth about mission trips is that you often go with one "mission" in mind, and in hindsight learn that your true mission was something completely different. This trip's mission was to teach me that my God is a big God whose care extends beyond the world I know. It was a humbling lesson, and a life-changing one.

The per capita annual GDP in Ethiopia is $251. That's less that my monthly car payment. By nearly every standard of Western measurement, the Ethiopians have it rough. Running water? If you're lucky. Air conditioning? What's that? A roof over your head? Made of tin.

Our Ethiopian friends would herd their own goats, which they'd later slaughter and eat for dinner. Forget Starbucks. They hand-ground and roasted the coffee beans for their afternoon espresso. They built homes with walls of mud and grass and welcomed us in, proudly. And they did it with smiles on their faces.

I've never been so humbled in my life.

The Ethiopians were fascinated with American culture. They wanted to know about our music and our politics and dating and they wanted to know how much things cost. How much was my jacket? My camera? How much does a house cost? It forces you to think and reassess when you realize that your most basic necessities are luxuries for others.

And there we were, a group of Americans, pretending to teach these joyful people about God. In reality, it was the other way around.

The thin place I experienced in Ethiopia showed me how God has blessed me and provided for me in ways I can never measure. Those creature comforts I take for granted, that I assume are essential for life, mean nothing in God's reality. Of course, I kind of knew that all along, but the experience there really drove it home.

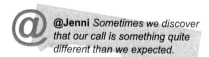

@Jenni *How can we carry our own "Ethiopias" with us all the time, humbled and mindful? It is so much bigger than any one of us.*

Before that trip, it had always been easy to think that being a good Christian was about assessing proper doctrine and giving the right percentage and saying the right things and avoiding the wrong ones, etc., etc., etc. In hindsight, that's a perspective that's All About Me. In Ethiopia, I saw that it's not. And in that experience, I learned a little more about walking humbly with my God.

●

Back to the whole idea of "call"...

I spend more time with myself than with anyone else. So, it's only natural that I might sometimes struggle to remember that *It's Not All About Me.* But Micah 6:8 and social justice and homeless folks in L.A. and my Ethiopian memories remind me that it's not. They remind me that I'm called to be part of a world that's a lot bigger than just my bubble. That I

@Jenni *Sometimes we discover that our call is something quite different than we expected.*

kinda think we're all called to do the same. That maybe the call takes different forms, and we can sometimes disagree on what those forms might be. But if our goal and our call is to minimize our own self-importance and maximize others'...well, I think the guy in Birkenstocks just might agree.

●

- Marc's conversation partner was Jennifer Fischer. She read Marc's essay and sent the tweets you see in the margins. Find Jenni's essay, "Coffee Can Change" on page 99.

Looking Around
Resource Suggestions from the Author and Editors

Sojourners Magazine—www.sojo.net

Charity: Water—www.charitywater.org

Disciples Crossing Camping Facility—www.disciplescrossing.org

Questions \ for Discussion and Contemplation

1 What does the concept of a "call" from God on your life mean to you? What is your call?

2 If you consider yourself to be a person of faith, does this make a difference in how you spend your money? Your time? Your vote?

3 Have you ever experienced a "thin place" as Istook describes it? What was that like for you?

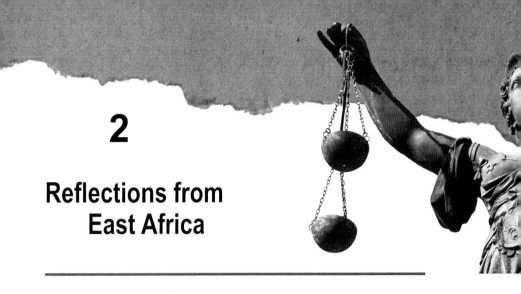

2

Reflections from East Africa

SHELVIS & NANCY SMITH-MATHER

[Nairobi, Kenya]

SHELVIS: If you ever want to rethink your life, talk with a seven year old. And if you need extra help, invite her five-year-old brother.

I recently made a video call to my niece and nephew, ages seven and five, respectively. The little ones squealed and giggled as the image of their "dancing" uncle shimmied across their computer screen in Atlanta. The seams of my navy blue blazer and charcoal slacks folded and stretched, as I spun in a swivel chair in my Nairobi office. Their caramel hands cupped their mouths to contain the laughter roaring from their bellies, while their joyful outbursts offered the sounds my ears yearned to hear. The encounter came on a day when I needed to be reminded of the lighter side of life. We all have those days, right? We need days when laughter soothes our weary spirits and wise counsel eases our troubled souls.

My wife and I have been living and serving in East Africa since 2008. Although we love our work, the separation from family is challenging. Recently, the situation has become more difficult, as my wife spends several months at a time in the Sudan while I remain in Kenya.

> **@Chloe** *Imagining the feelings of isolation reminds me of the strength and courage it takes to place others before ourselves, and ourselves closer to God.*

[Rural South Sudan]

NANCY: One of my Sudanese co-workers explained to me that injustice is about people who are rich and powerful not wanting others to be like them. Although he was not directing his statement at me, I felt personally convicted by his words.

Only 33 percent of people in the world can read, only 7 percent access the Internet, and 1 percent receive a college education.[1] I am literate, connected to the World Wide Web, and college educated. In addition, I am a thirty-year-old, European-American woman. My ethnicity gives me influence in my country, and my nationality grants me authority on the world stage. When I ignore the injustices in my hometown of Atlanta, or in my current residence in Southern Sudan, I am the one who is keeping others down. It is me.

If you are reading this book, you are obviously literate. Either you or a person you are connected with has enough disposable income to purchase reading material for leisure, which is significant considering more than one-half of the people in the world live on less than $2 a day.[2] So, I assume you join me in a position of privilege, and I hope you are also my companion in asking what to do with it.

We wrestle, we discern, we wonder: "What does it mean for us to act justly in our current situations?"

SHELVIS: Two weeks ago, Nancy and I celebrated our fifth wedding anniversary. There was no bouquet of flowers, dinner, or dancing. We didn't watch our wedding video together or look through old photo albums. Instead, we shared a long distance Internet conversation fraught with static and interspersed with "I love you"... *crick-crackle-crack*..."I miss you." Her hushed tones were barely audible from the barley brown mud hut in south Sudan. The anniversary was a harsh reminder of the sometimes isolating nature of our work. We chose to laugh, although it would have been easy to cry.

@Joe *Separation can breed anxiety, but you guys show true strength when you surpass it to fulfill something much bigger.*

My niece and nephew knew about all of the challenges, yet they chose to respond with hope. They knew Uncle Shelvis and Aunt Nancy were in different places in Africa. They knew "Mom-Mom" (my mother) was sick. They even knew that I was going to miss "Pop-Pop's" (my father's) upcoming birthday celebration. Nevertheless, they focused less on the problems and more on the possibility in the situation. They assured me of "Mom-Mom's" quick recovery, pledged to bear-hug "Pop-Pop" on my behalf, and they affectionately smeared the computer with half-a-dozen tiny kisses. They explained that the kisses should be given to my wife when I see her again. Our conversation only lasted a few minutes, but their words lifted my spirits and helped me re-evaluate my life.

My niece and nephew reminded me of the transformative power of hope. Hope calls us to acknowledge the present challenges of life, while also recognizing the potential that lies ahead. To paraphrase the author of the book of Hebrews: "Faith is being sure of what we hope for and certain of what we do not see." This "faith" is rooted in the belief that God can improve any situation. People of faith are called to maintain this perspective when engaging the world. We are called to fully assess our surroundings and believe things can change for the better.

@Chloe *I completely agree, Shelvis. Hope can transform! Step back, reflect on our present situation, and move forward.*

NANCY: At present, I work with a team of Sudanese colleagues to facilitate churches and communities working together to improve their lives. Sudan's civil war, which lasted over twenty years, killed 1.5 million people and dismantled the infrastructure in the southern region of the country. After the signing of the Comprehensive Peace Agreement in 2005, the war between the north and south ended, and millions of southern Sudanese returned home.[3] They found that years of conflict had weakened local institutions, including churches, and there was need to rebuild.

In response to the trauma of war and dependence on foreign assistance, our program is designed to help participants identify and use locally available resources to meet their community's needs. When congregations join the program, our team facilitates an "envisioning" process for the church leaders. We begin with Bible studies that show God's desire for church members to be both spiritually and physically healthy. Then together we try to understand the church's role in helping their local community develop holistically.

In one Bible study, we read the miracle of Jesus feeding five thousand people. According to the gospel of Mark (6:30–44), on a particular day Jesus taught many things until it was late.

Consequently, the disciples told Jesus to send the hungry crowd home to search for food. "You give them something to eat," Jesus responded to the disciples. He challenged them to go and see what food they already had with them. They found five loaves and two fish. Jesus took the disciples' small resources, blessed and shared them with the large group. The entire crowd ate and they were satisfied. (Mark 6:30-44)

SHELVIS: My wife and I believe the church plays a critical role in restoring hope in a world often filled with despair. Several years ago, we applied to the Young Adult Volunteer Program of the Presbyterian Church (USA) because we wanted to participate in the work of the church internationally. As a result, I serve an organization called the Fellowship of Christian Councils & Churches in the Great Lakes & Horn of Africa (FECCLAHA). This organization was created in response to cross-border conflicts and works to enhance peace and reconciliation in the Great Lakes and Horn of Africa. The organization helps churches and church councils in nine countries address the region's political, gender, ethnic, religious, and land conflicts.[4] In other words, they assess the challenges in the region and choose to respond with hope.

Some mornings, before the sun's rusty auburn rays cut through the mosquito net covering my bed, I ask myself, "How in the world did I end up in Africa?" Seriously. I was content with my life and job in the United States. I loved living in Atlanta. In fact, when Nancy first approached me with the idea of the Young Adult Volunteer Program, I quieted her inquiry by responding, "Let's pray about it." What I meant was, "Let's never talk about this ever, ever again." Something, however, changed inside of me. Maybe it was the recognition that life is about more than just my desires and comfort. Maybe it was the realization that everyone longs for the healing message of hope, and the people of East Africa are no exception.

NANCY: "We are just like the disciples," a local Pastor said to me, "we think we have nothing." All the participants agreed. So, I asked each person in the meeting to identify one thing they were good at, one thing God allows them to do well.

Their answers were awesome: "teaching children," "welcoming visitors," "helping people who are arguing reconcile with each other," "preaching," "preparing food," "helping the needy," "visiting people in prison," "forgiving," "sharing food with the hungry," "teaching our mother tongue," "praying for the sick," "working hard for personal improvement," "doing well in school," and "farming." I wrote each response down, and then read the entire list back to the group. Smiles captured downcast faces. Those gathered recognized that, even if their gifts seemed small or insignificant, God could use those resources to do great things in their community.

After the series of Bible studies, the church leaders develop a vision for their church. Then they work together with community leaders to identify local needs and resources and devise an action plan for development. A committee of community and church members is elected and trained, and then oversees the implementation of the plan. In addition to using local resources, the committee, once it becomes well organized, is able to network with other communities, organizations, and the local government to leverage resources, information, and skills to carry out its plan.

One community may decide its greatest need is education, so it uses local resources to build a school. Another may focus on starting savings and loans groups or increasing agricultural productivity to fight hunger. Whatever the direction, it is determined through the discernment of the church and community, implemented by the committee, supported by the local community, and often carried out in partnership with others.

SHELVIS: This region of the world has endured a great deal of conflict and tragedy during the past decade. Kenya is still recovering from the political and ethnic violence of 2007 and 2008 following the contested presidential and general elections. The disputes resulted in the internal displacement of over 300,000 people and the deaths of over fifteen hundred. However, the disharmony present in surrounding countries is even more daunting. Outbreaks of fighting continue in Democratic Republic of Congo (DRC) at an alarming rate despite the presence of the world's largest United Nations peacekeeping force. The Congolese death toll within the last decade is more than the combined fatalities in the 9/11 tragedy, the invasion of Iraq and the Persian Gulf War. Further instability is evident in Uganda's continued deferral of the Juba Peace agreement, which is critical to a nation plagued by militia violence. Sudan's fragile Comprehensive Peace Agreement between Northern and Southern Sudan becomes even more worrisome as the nation endures one of the greatest humanitarian tragedies in recent history. As a result of Darfur and other national conflicts, hundreds of thousands of Sudanese have been killed by war and disease, while over 3 million individuals have been displaced from their homes.[5]

NANCY: My hope in participating in this program in Boma, Sudan, is that no one in this community will ever die again of diarrhea caused by dirty drinking water and a lack of medicine; that young boys will no longer wear wooden carved guns over their shoulders, imitating the soldiers who are ever-present in their town; that in the small village called Naoyapuru, a young girl aspiring to be a pilot will not be limited by cultural obstacles to the education of girls, and will learn to fly.

Living in Sudan comes with high highs and low lows. Those are some of the highs. Let me share some lows:

For an urban young adult living in a rural setting, one day is like a week. Boma lacks a cell phone network, so I am isolated from familiar voices that bring me comfort. Without an interpreter, I struggle to communicate with the local people, so most conversations are limited to greetings. Also, attitudes towards women in this area are so far from my experience in the States, I am often caught off-guard. I don't even know how to respond to a male colleague who makes statements like, "God intended for women to wear skirts," "Women should not play soccer," or "Women can't do things effectively."

In Sudan, I am confronted daily with the huge gap between wealth and poverty that exists in our world. The divide is always present with me. I am continually asked for clothes, food, school fees, and medicine. At times the people look to me for a word of encouragement from Scripture, as many people here are illiterate and don't have a Bible in their native language.

In addition, more than once, my white arm has been placed next to that of a woman in Boma, and my color has been described as "good" while the darker-skinned arm was labeled "bad." In such moments, I experience intense and sharp feelings of guilt and anger knowing that people "like me" taught and perpetuated that lesson in this area. A deep sense of mourning weighs on my spirit each time I realize how many people here have internalized that oppressive and painful message. I struggle with all of this and more. With no television and often no electrical power, I have a lot of time for my thoughts to battle within my head.

@Joe Nancy, your work speaks to an ideal: to fight fire with love, and inequality and despair with compassion.

SHELVIS: I am currently co-editor of a project with theologians from Africa and North America aimed at developing a "Contextual Bible Study Manual on Peace Building and Reconciliation." The aim of this project is to create a theological tool to help people address issues of community discord. The manual allows participants to explore biblical stories of conflict as a way of better understanding their own experiences of violence.

NANCY: In my down moments, I find myself asking God, "What is your will for me in this place?"

If I am walking with God, I realize my lowly position in God's presence, my great ability when aided by God's strength, and my equal status with each person I encounter. When I live with my local and global neighbors according to those truths, then I reflect my connection with a compassionate God. While living in Boma, I see clearly that it is in the depth of God's all-encompassing love that matters of justice, mercy, and humility make sense. God loves the people here unconditionally, so I am called to do the same.

There is power that comes from realizing what God wants us to do. The potential to carry out good works that transform local communities, and eventually the world, is realized when people labor together within a family, a village, a country, and across the globe. I am extremely honored to be part of what God is doing in and through the churches in Southern Sudan.

SHELVIS: In putting together the previously mentioned Bible study resource, I also incorporated the voices of "ordinary" citizens who have led extraordinary efforts in bringing about reconciliation. This section was my favorite to compile because I learned from young adults whose courage and resilience provide a model for people around the world.

- Jean Paul Gitali, a twenty-five-year-old survivor of genocide from Rwanda, taught me about the power of forgiveness. He lost sixty family members during the 1994 conflict, yet he maintains that harboring anger only perpetuates a cycle of destruction.

- Michael Kimanda Spoon, a former child soldier in Sudan, taught me that a person's past has no bearing on his or her future. He was stolen from his family at the age of ten and forced into a militia group, but he is now in school with the goal of improving the legal system of his country.

- The young women and men from Nzumari African Art taught me that the gifts of dance and drama are a powerful means to bring about peace. In the slums of Nairobi, they staged puppet shows and culture dance exhibitions to bring community members together in discussion groups. Once gathered together, they talked about their differences, which helped them to resist joining the riots of 2007 and 2008.

Just as these young adults used their passions and gifts to transform their circumstances in East Africa, young adults in every part of the world are uniquely positioned to do the same. Our obligation to a better humanity and world necessitates the work of our hearts, hands, and minds.

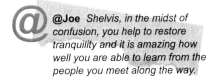

@Joe *Shelvis, in the midst of confusion, you help to restore tranquility and it is amazing how well you are able to learn from the people you meet along the way.*

So let us make the most of what lies before us and within us, so that our faith makes the unseen possibilities into realities.

NANCY: When I see that a new vision of what is possible can transform one person, it motivates me to push beyond my own, self-created limitations. When someone whose hand I touch realizes his or her personal value is the same as that of a *khawajah* (foreigner), I know my presence here is significant.

May God grant us all moments when we glimpse what the world would be like if we truly act justly, love constantly, and walk in humility. May we have the courage to believe we are able to overcome the injustices

@Chloe *Inspired to continue on my faith journey, searching for what God is calling me to do with my life, to glorify God to the fullest.*

hiding in the corners of our own lives and crying out to us from around the world. May we live up to the calling on our lives, for the glory of God.

●

● Shelvis and Nancy's conversation partners were Joe Geoghegan and Chloe Grammer. They read Shelvis and Nancy's essay and sent the tweets you see in the margins. Find Joe & Chloe's essay, "Camp Bani" on page 52.

Looking Around
Resource Suggestions from the Author and Editors

Nancy & Shelvis, From Georgia to Kenya
  http://nancyandshelvis.com

PC(USA) Young Adult Volunteer Program
  http://gamc.pcusa.org/ministries/yav/

Across—http://across-sudan.org/

Church World Service—http://www.churchworldservice.org

Notes

[1]Family Care Foundation. Available at: http://www.familycare.org/special-interest/if-the-world-were-a-village-of-100-people/

[2]Population Reference Bureau. Available at: http://www.prb.org/Journalists/PressReleases/2005/

[3]BBC Country Profile. Available at: http://news.bbc.co.uk/2/hi/middle_east/country_profiles/ 820864.stm

[4]The organization's membership includes national councils and other regional church structures in Burundi, Democratic Republic of the Congo, Eritrea, Ethiopia, Kenya, Rwanda, Sudan, Tanzania, and Uganda.

[5]BBC Country Profile. Available at: http://news.bbc.co.uk/2/hi/820864.stmMoreThanHalf theWorldLivesonLessThan2aDayAugust2005.aspx

Questions \ for Discussion and Contemplation

1 What did you know about Kenya or Sudan before reading this essay? Have your impressions or perceptions of these countries and their people changed at all?

2 What does forgiveness mean to you? Can you imagine offering the kind of forgiveness Jean Paul Gitali has extended to those who murdered his family?

3 Where do you see injustice in your own life? Does it matter?

3

A War on Two Fronts

JOSHUA DOBBS

"So how did you end up choosing to go into the service?" she asked, a little more than a week before I left for my year away.

"I don't know. I guess I just tend to do the things that most others can't or won't."

I'm certainly no angel, but somehow I have managed to end up in fields that are of a service nature. I'll admit the initial reasons are not necessary altruistic, but the personal growth and lessons in serving have certainly been the reward.

Whether competing in triathlons; completing a master's degree; obtaining my pilot's license; building my own computers; joining the Army; practicing Tae Kwon Do and yoga; or learning to tile, plumb, and wire my own house, I like being the "can do it" guy. When people say, "You can do that?" I like being able to say "Yes." The most frustrating thing about this is that there are clearly not enough hours in the day to work fulltime, maintain any form of social and family life, and be proficient at all of these things simultaneously. So I ride a roller coaster of conflicted priorities, feeling I never achieve my "best" in any one area.

More to the point, I'm not much of a writer and I am admittedly a boring storyteller–but that's why we have editors! And while I'm skeptical that my thoughts and viewpoints (decidedly agnostic) will find a happy synergy in a series called "Where's the Faith?" I know the importance of teamwork and mentoring, of sharing stories, and of achieving feelings of strength, success, and growth.

"Onward now you Cardinals"

As a junior at Ball State, I had a fraternity brother in the Army National Guard. He was a young sergeant and spoke highly of his time in "The Guard." While the benefits (and the associated risks) are much higher for young people now, at the time he was getting roughly $300.00 a month in drill pay and educational benefits—a fortune to me at the time! My best friend and I talked about going into some sort of reserve component service that would allow us to finish school and live mostly civilian lives while still serving and making some cash on the side. We both had girlfriends and pretty pleasant, if frugal, lives and didn't consider fulltime service to be an option.

Just to be clear, early on, when I was a twenty year old, making twenty year old decisions, it *was* all about me. I asked recruiters: What would I get out of it? How much money would I make? How long would I be out of school? How much training would I be required to complete? What were the benefits to me? Wearing the uniform was a "cool" thought and, in some as-yet-undefined way, the thought of "serving my country" sounded good. I spoke with Army, Marine, Air Force, and Navy recruiters. I weighed the scales of which branch of service and military specialty could benefit me the most.

"Which job gives the highest signing bonus?" I asked selfishly. "Infantry," the recruiter replied. "Fine. I'll do that then." I had no real concept of what that meant or the training I would go through to be an "infantryman," but, hey, it paid the highest bonus, right? The process of changing into a soldier proudly serving and holding himself to higher personal standard was gradual…diffuse—certainly not a straight shot.

From Bonus to Basic

Some of the concepts in basic training were foreign to me. Being an only child, I had always only been responsible for myself. In basic training, no task is done correctly until the entire platoon completes it correctly. I was held accountable for the failures of others (and they for mine). We lived these lessons in the Georgia summer heat, getting sweaty, exercising to physical exhaustion, being "lovingly" barked at by drill sergeants. Successful completion of the assigned task was the minimum standard, and you didn't get warm fuzzies or pats on the back for simply *meeting the standard.*

The absence of reprimand was reward enough in that environment. Hearing, "At least you finished without messing up, Turd," or the coveted "Nice shot" from a drill sergeant was like gold. In a civilian society (and generation) where we are constantly told that we are special, and that as long as we "try"—regardless of the outcome—it will be "okay," this cut-and-dried reality check was a real eye opener for a young man. I probably don't give those experiences enough credit for how they have shaped me over the years. As cold as this may sound, there are times in life I've had to remember: either you can "cut it," or you can't. For most of us, "not cutting it" means what? Less money? Not as nice a house? A crummy car? In the military context, it means you end up dead, and in the process you probably took some of your buddies and, potentially, an entire way of life with you.

No pressure, Private!

Into the Sandbox

Over my time in the Guard, I transitioned from infantry soldier to cavalry scout in Texas, and eventually into a role as a signal soldier. It was with a signal unit, the 138th Signal Battalion, that I was deployed to spend a year in Ramadi, Iraq. Signal is the Army's version of the phone and Internet guys. Secured voice and data communications are a huge portion of a modern battlefield operation and, though I wasn't kicking in doors like I would have as an infantry soldier, I felt that successfully completing my mission in Iraq saved lives and supported the greater mission overall. As we always said, "Signal: You can talk about us, but you can't talk without us."

In Iraq, my team of six soldiers was responsible for installing and maintaining 24/7 secured voice and data services for our medical hospital, our civil affairs group, our postal service, the psychological operations group, the maintenance group, the water purification group, and the heavy equipment operators.

We helped make it possible for medical care to be provided, projects to be initiated with local contractors, letters to get to and from homesick troops, the hearts and minds of (some) locals to be won, Humvees to be repaired, water to be made drinkable, and tons of supplies and equipment to be loaded and unloaded.

Over the thirteen years I served in the Guard, I ultimately gained a respect for the importance of a smaller role in a larger context. Our individual actions can have rippling consequences—both positive and negative—on the whole. Learning from my superiors, my team, and my time with the Guard, I know that every decision I make now in my "regular" life might affect the lives of others (including other living things on the planet, not just humans). Like I said, I'm no angel, but awareness is a starting point and I strive to grow more aware of my impact as time goes on.

@**Erika** *A lesson in humility and being content to do what's right without the need for honor, glory, or personal acknowledgment.*

From Combat to Care

Heart disease is the number one killer of Americans each year. Obesity and diabetes are epidemics that make the swine flu panic pale in comparison in terms of human lives lost. We are an incredibly shortsighted and unhealthy population overall. The things we consistently choose to put in our bodies and the lack of effort we put into being fit are staggering. I truly believe in loving people for who they are, and not focusing exclusively on the physical aspects of our existence as the sole metric of worth. At the same time, I find the utter lack of respect the average American has for his or her own body—and the ability it has to carry the important "what's inside" through a normal, functional life—almost incomprehensible.

Of course, I didn't always know these things or feel this way. In college, I was a young athlete and could eat an entire large pizza without blinking. Powdered donuts were the breakfast of choice, and a bag of nacho chips seemed like a perfectly reasonable dinner choice. I really didn't get a clue until I decided on a major. I had tried initial stints as a nursing major, then, as a natural resources major, but eventually I found a home in the study of exercise science.

[*rant*] I know, I know. I am fully aware of the stigma associated with any educational endeavor associated with "physical" or "exercise" in the title. I find it interesting that a finance graduate who gathers financial data, manipulates variables, motivates clients, and guides behaviors to save or make money is respected at a level bordering on reverence… but when I change the statement to an exercise science graduate who gathers physical data, manipulates variables, motivates clients and guides behaviors to save or add years of quality *life*, it doesn't get the same response. [*end of rant*]

As an exercise science major, I gradually learned more about the human body, how it functions, and that a bag of nacho chips probably wasn't a good choice for dinner. Though not a stellar undergraduate student, I was able to make the cut for graduate study at Baylor University, and I spent two more years going deeper into the science of health, wellness, and human performance. As a culminating experience for my graduate study, I was awarded an excellent internship in the cardiac rehabilitation program at the Hillcrest Baptist Medical Center near Baylor.

I was able to work with individuals who had experienced heart attacks, balloon angioplasty, stent placement, coronary bypass surgery, and even heart transplant surgery. This was such an eye opener, and provided a tremendous connection between the lessons I had learned in the classroom and the affects our lifestyles have on our bodies. We were responsible for helping these heart patients recover more fully and return to functional lives at the level they had enjoyed prior to their events—often even higher! When I graduated, I was offered a job at the hospital doing the work that I had grown to love.

Immediately after I graduated and while working at the hospital, I considered continuing my education in the medical field and began taking classes on my lunch breaks and evenings to prepare myself for medical or physician's assistant school. Instead, I was drawn back to my alma mater, Ball State, and spent eight years with the university (with the deployment consuming some time in there) teaching in, and developing the curriculum for, the exercise science major I had graduated from!

If you, as a student, ever sat in a class and thought to yourself, "I could teach this," or, "It couldn't be that hard"…well, let me just say: I'll never, ever say that I always knew what I was doing, or that I never got caught without a good answer, but I sure learned a lot more *teaching* exercise science than I ever did being a student.

Now, as the manager of non-invasive cardiology at a large Midwestern hospital, I lead a team of approximately sixty people. Our staff includes the IV/EKG, echocardiography, cardiac surveillance, and cardiac rehabilitation programs. Just like my signal days with the Guard, we're there making everything work together. When Methodist Hospital was named among America's Best, we were part of that. Most of the time—on a military field or in the medical one—you pay more attention when things *don't* work; when all is working, as it should, there's often little praise to be found. So to have our team recognized among the best in our field is quite an honor.

Like anyone, when I was young and unaware I had no idea that the choices I was making everyday could kill me: some sooner, some later. Now, with years of experience and learning, I know that my staff and I are only there because people need us. Sometimes the patients have made decisions that have led their bodies to fail, and they need us to motivate, encourage, and empower them to regain health and function. Sometimes, a body just doesn't work like it should, and those people need us too. Either way, our task is to treat and improve.

@Erika *A medical team that doesn't pass judgment on patients and focuses on the bigger picture: better quality of life. Yes!*

Turning the Corner

"So what does that part of your life (the Guard) have to do with your life now?" she asked.

The discipline and bearing of the military taught me to take charge of my life. Accomplishing what you didn't think you could, while knowing that others are counting on you, is a huge lesson to learn, and sometimes you learn it the hard way. Now, every day, my goal is the personal recovery of any individual in our care, and our systems have to work together to

@**Erika** *It's comforting to know that there are still people in the medical field for the right reasons.*

make that happen. I hope that by participating in work that educates and empowers people, I can help in some small way to change the tide of unnecessary chronic illness. I hope people will learn to live well.

●

● Josh's conversation partner was Erika Roman Saint-Pierre. She read Josh's essay and sent the tweets you see in the margins. Find Erika's essay, "Difference Makes a Difference," on page 42.

Questions \for Discussion and \Contemplation

1 What are the "rippling consequences" of your life as you live it now?

2 Who in your life counts on you? Who do you count on?

3 Are you living well? What is the impact of *not* living well on others around you?

4

Legacy, Responsibility, and Faith

KENDRA DUNBAR

When I was a child, Holy Week—Palm Sunday, Maundy Thursday, Good Friday *Tenebrae* service, and last, but most certainly not least, Easter—was of great importance. Worship services, choir rehearsal, liturgical dance practice, serving as an acolyte, dyeing Easter eggs—all of it meant family together. It was church, a week of faith and community, and I always loved it.

Next to Christmas and Easter, the service that stood out the most to me was Maundy Thursday. In my church, Maundy Thursday concluded with a foot washing ceremony. I think it was the ritualized experience of actually washing the feet of whoever happened to be sitting next to me (I would now call this experiential learning) that stood out the most. It gave the service and the day deeper meaning. It exemplified the importance of humility in service, and at a very young age I somehow understood that lesson. Allowing whoever it was that was sitting on the other side of me to wash my feet exemplified trust, caring, and connection through the shared moment so sacred in faith communities. The reciprocity of the action—I wash your feet, you wash mine—spoke to principles of equity and solidarity in relationship. These profoundly important tenets piqued my interest as a girl and became fundamental to my faith understanding and practice as I grew older.

Maundy Thursday made me think, feel, and experience. Easter morning brought with it unbridled enthusiasm. Most

Sundays my father stayed home, but Easter morning we knew even Dad was coming to church. We would all have breakfast together, then put on our Easter best—which for me meant black patent leather shoes and white tights (if it wasn't quite warm enough for sandals), a new or newly handed-down pretty dress, an Easter bonnet, and sometimes even little white gloves. I would put my Easter basket on my arm, my brother and I would have our picture taken in front of the house, and then we were off to church. Easter was the celebration, but there was something about the preparation and ritual of Holy Week that made Easter even more exciting. It was the calm before the party, the lessons that had to be learned before graduation day. My mother was full of lessons, especially lessons of faith and morality, which she carefully instilled in my brother and me from the time we were quite small. I would later learn that handing down faith—how to live, how to behave, and whom we serve—was an established family tradition. My mother, then a teacher, always made time to work with us at home to supplement what we were learning from school, church, our friends, and television.

Throughout my childhood, my family participated in rallies and marches in Washington, D.C. Ending Apartheid, cutting spending on nuclear weapons, justice in Palestine, ending racism, creating better jobs and livable wages, and promoting women's equal rights were some of the causes to which we lent our voices, spirits, and Saturdays. The majority of our "home schooling" coincided with holidays and celebrations. During Black History month, we watched segments of documentaries and listened to the Student Non-Violent Coordinating Committee Freedom Singers. Lessons would be on ancestors and leaders such as Sojourner Truth, Mary McCloud Bethune, Malcolm X, the Black Panthers, Shirley Chisholm, Nelson Mandela, and Gandhi. We watched *Eyes on the Prize* and *Cry Freedom*.

During that month we also participated in all kinds of community events. My brother and I would have to write poems that we would read aloud at the Black History celebration at the library, and sing freedom songs at various events. Before Dr. Martin Luther King's birthday was a national holiday, my mother would take us out of school to honor his life. We would spend the day looking at her old photographs of the movement, reading about King, hearing her stories of community organizing in Newark and Alabama, and learning more about the man and the movement that surrounded him. The best part of the day was reading the telegram Dr. King sent to her on March 5, 1968 (less than one month before he was murdered). The telegram recognized her as a leader and invited her to a special meeting to establish "joint thinking" around the Poor People's Campaign. With that telegram, my mother was placed in history. I felt incredibly connected to previous struggles for freedom, equality under the law, and justice for all communities. I could place my mother in history, and therefore I could place myself in history. The legacy of my ancestors, the legacy of legendary leaders who fought for peace and justice, the legacy of my mother stood before me as inspiration. The question was, where would that inspiration lead me?

I remember Good Friday as the day when the sacred became inextricably connected to the legacies of those who inspired me. On Good Friday, my mother supplemented our Sunday school lessons with thought-provoking discussion and action. She didn't just want us to memorize Bible stories; she wanted us to understand what they meant and how we were called to live. My mother knew if we found meaning in the stories and could make applications to our lives, we were much more likely to live lives guided by biblical scripture. So, on Good Friday my brother, mother, and I sat down and talked about what the day signified. She would review the events of the Passion story, and then ask us to reflect on how Jesus lived his life. *What did he do while he was alive? What do the stories and parables tell us?*

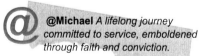

@**Michael** *A lifelong journey committed to service, emboldened through faith and conviction.*

How should we live our lives? We would talk about the power of faith, the importance of believing in something and being guided by those beliefs.

We would also talk about the cost of living a life guided by your beliefs. On Good Friday Jesus was crucified for the life he led while on earth. He was crucified for living his beliefs. As children, my brother and I saw clearly the commonality between the example that Jesus' life provided us and the reality that both Dr. Martin Luther King Jr. and Mahatma Gandhi died as a result of a very public commitment to living out their faith. That connection taught me that I did not have to be divine to pattern my life after Christ's teachings. After a good theological discussion with a six and nine year old, my mother would sum up with something like this:

So, today is Good Friday. Since today reminds us of the day Jesus was sacrificed on the cross, today is a day when we should remember what he lived for. Jesus lived for others. He helped children, women, and poor people. He stood up when he saw those in power use their power to hurt others. What do you want to stand up for? What issue do you care about? One way to stand up is to make your voice heard. Would you like to write to President Reagan to tell him what you are thinking about this Good Friday? What do you need to tell the President?

At age six, I wrote:

Dear President Reagan,
I am in first grade. I wish that you wouldn't spend so much on weapons. I wish you would spend more money for helping others. I want all children to have enough food and clothing. It scares me when you let bombs go on other countries. I think Jesus wouldn't want our country to spend so much on bombs and weapons.
Thank you,
Kendra Dunbar

(See actual letter on next page.)

What I love about this letter is that it is clear that my six-year-old self wrote it, backward letters and all. I wrote this letter from the heart, without hesitation, completely unselfconscious and completely unaware that not every six year old wrote letters to the President on Good Friday. I wrote what I knew: that too much money was spent on weapons. I wrote what I wanted: all children to have food and clothing. And I wrote what I felt:

Kendra Dunbar - Age 6
9476 Timesweep Lane
Columbia, Md. 21045
April 1, 1983 Good Friday

Dear President Reagan,
I am in first grade. I wish that you wouldn't spend so much on weapons. I wish you would spend more money for helping others. I want all children to have enough food and clothing. It scares me when you let bombs go on other countries. I think Jesus wouldn't want our country to spend so much on bombs and weapons.

thank you,
Kendra Dunbar

Copies: Senator Sarbanes
Senator Mathias
Congresswoman Mikulski

scared that bombs were being dropped on other countries. I even alluded to my own little theological understanding that Jesus wouldn't want our country to spend so much on weapons. By the age of six my faith had taught me that Jesus wanted peace, and spending a lot of money on weapons did not make for peace.

I understood Jesus to be the son of God who was sent to teach us lessons of peace and justice. I heard about the lion lying down with the lamb. I knew about the prodigal son, the good Samaritan, the woman at the well, and the beatitudes. I understood that Jesus would want all children to be alive, with enough food and clothing. I understood that to honor the Jesus that I loved I had to write to Reagan and share what I knew. I thought my letter could help him make decisions. I thought I could make an impact. Unfortunately, I did not get a reply to my letter.

My brother, Dedrick, did receive a picture of President Reagan dressed up like a cowboy sitting on a horse with a smile and a wave. I'll never forget how hurt and angry he was. He didn't want that picture. *He wanted a response to his concern.* I remember the lessons of that Good Friday ritual. I remember talking with my mother about peace. I remember believing in myself. I remember feeling important because I was taking a stand. But I also remember the hurt, determination, and disappointment in my brother's voice. "Did they even read it?" he asked. "Did they read my letter?" That frustration and confusion was an early lesson for me in the sting of feeling ignored, unseen, and unheard. It was an early lesson for me in the wisdom and strategy of the persistent widow.

@**Michael** *What is faith without action? A testament to the importance of not only publically, but radically, living out one's faith.*

Today, instead of choosing a topic for a letter to the president, I have to choose a career, a vocation, a way of life, and companions with whom I will share my life. Currently, I work for a mainline Protestant denomination. Officially, I am the Executive of Global Youth Networks. Practically, that means I work with young people all over the world. The agency I work for is an international church body that is in mission all over the world and is one of many institutions and organizations that work toward alleviating the symptoms and addressing the root causes of poverty. It is my job to engage young people in programs, projects, and mission that incorporate direct service models while focusing on the work of justice, advocacy, and theological reflection. My job is to create space for young people to dialogue with one another, analyze their contexts, create plans for community engagement, become exposed to and learn from resource people from their own countries and regions, and develop and participate in mission grounded in principles of justice and Christian teachings.

Due to the global nature of my work and the diversity of the church, my office engages many critical social issues. A prevailing issue for young people in all regions and from many divergent demographics is the issue of violence, in all its forms: interpersonal to economic, gendered to national conflicts, hatred to physical abuse, multilateral war to emotional violence. Gun violence, violence against women, war, violence in schools (or while on your way there), sex trade, street violence, rape, extrajudicial killings, violence in the home, racism and hate, dating violence, heterosexism and gender violence: violence in all its forms hurts, stifles, and disempowers young people. I work with young people to envision, plan, and strategize a response to the violence. We design community education programs and missions of exchange and exposure to cultivate dialogue and understanding. The young people work locally to reintegrate child soldiers, to campaign for more just sentencing laws, to advocate for the rights of overseas domestic workers, to rebuild communities after severe natural disasters, to create spaces of healing for survivors of rape and war, and to confront community stereotypes that lead to discrimination, segregation, and acts of violence.

@**@Michael** *From the humility of the feet washing basins of Maundy Thursday to engaging youth daily on a global basis, you embody the spirit of Jesus Christ.*

The lessons of my childhood informed by my journey to adulthood shape how I interact with young people. In some respects, I have an odd and at times seemingly overwhelming job. I serve young people all over the world. We debate social issues, discuss lived realities, explore global and local root causes of poverty and violence, analyze local and global policy, and develop understanding of the history and legacy of Christianity and mission. We do all of this so that together we can develop mission and ministries that seek to educate, accompany, and empower local communities. We pray together, learn church polity, sing, dance, laugh, and seek and find deeper connections with God through Bible studies and engaging in theologies that liberate. We do a lot together. It is the most glorious and fulfilling work, but the reality is I can never do it all. The work is never finished. Life and faith are a journey.

Good Friday still is a most sacred and meaningful time for me, and I have to attribute this to the early lessons my mother taught us and the legacy of faith and commitment that guides my path. Good Friday is a day that grounds me. It is the time when I really feel called to account for my faith and to atone for the ways I have faltered or just not truly lived out my faith with passion and conviction. Good Friday is the day when God's love and Jesus' sacrifice are the most palpable for me. I am always humbled, and I must continually recommit myself to living out a righteous faith, one that keeps me in right and balanced relationship with creation and the Creator. When I look back, I realize that the early lessons that I was taught and the traditions my family shared have caused me to ground my faith in the prophetic. To believe is beautiful, but to live what you believe, *that* is faith I hope to embody.

●

● Kendra's conversation partner was Michael Wagner. He read Kendra's essay and sent the tweets you see in the margins. Find Michael's essay, "Current City: ____" on page 59.

Looking Around
Resource Suggestions from the Author and Editors

Eyes on the Prize (PBS Home Video 1987)
A documentary about the American civil rights movement from 1952 to 1965.

Cry Freedom (Universal Pictures 1987)
South African journalist Donald Woods (Kevin Kline) is forced to flee the country after attempting to investigate the death in custody of his friend, the black activist Steve Biko (Denzel Washington).

Legacy, Responsibility, and Faith

Questions \ for Discussion and Contemplation

1 What's your personal legacy? Your family history? Who have you been taught to be?

2 Who or what is your inspiration? Where does this lead you?

3 What does it mean to you to walk humbly with God—how would making a conscious effort to do this change your life?

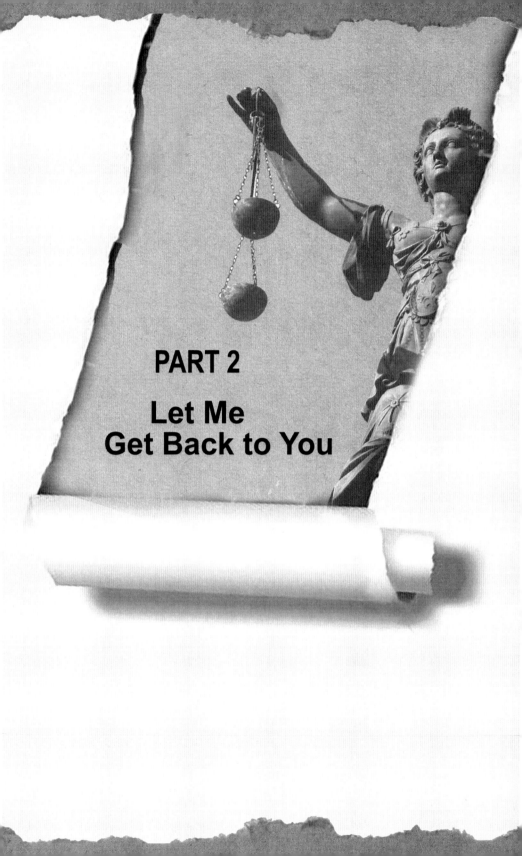

PART 2

**Let Me
Get Back to You**

5

Difference Makes
a Difference

ERIKA ROMAN SAINT-PIERRE

Difference Makes a Difference

Last night I had a dream.
It wasn't a good dream.
I guess you could call it a nightmare.
I lived in a world where everyone was the same.
A world where people all looked,
thought and acted the same;
and that was what was expected.
This world had rules without exceptions
and constraints were walls that could not yield.
In this world, where difference made a difference,
I alone was different.
My thoughts were my own,
and my countenance did not conform.
I searched in vain for my place in this world, and realized
when one walks to the beat of a different drum,
life can be a lonely journey.
When one walks to the beat of a different drum,
it can be a dangerous, desolate walk
through a land where safe harbors do not exist.

Erika Roman Saint-Pierre, age 14

As a young girl, I was plagued with myriads of problems fueled by inhibition, lack of confidence, and diffidence. I was different in monumental ways.

Being one of the only African-American students in my school, the color of my skin was a beacon that singled me out for observation. My religion—or more accurately, my mother's religion—set me apart from a society that seemed incapable of acceptance and understanding. Being seen as one of Jehovah's Witnesses made me stand out on two counts, both racially *and* religiously. My father, who had no religion, worshiped money, power and himself. The painful effect of emotional and physical abuse at his hand left me bereft in a world of affectation.

My story began in the early 1970's, on the east side of Indianapolis. My mother was a homemaker and a brilliant young woman. The adjectives people most often used to describe her were *beautiful* and *loving*, but, also, she was seriously moody and, as far back as I could recall, somewhat strange. My father was an up-and-coming technician in the burgeoning computer industry. Everyone agreed; he was a *genius*. To all appearances, we were the picture-perfect suburban, upwardly mobile family. By the time I was in kindergarten, it was obvious we were going places, and, even at that young age, I was somewhat aware of the esteem we'd gained. People envied us. But those were outward appearances, and had little to do with the reality of our lives behind the scenes.

The reality was...by first grade I'd been raped in my father's presence—and with his consent—by a neighbor. By second grade, it was obvious to me that in many ways, my mother was different from the mothers of my friends. The beautiful mother who loved me so much, at times *didn't* love me, and sometimes didn't know me at all. She started to disappear for hours and then days at a time. She would always return, often looking dismayed and confused, but without explanation.

My father introduced me to alcohol before I was five. The first time I got drunk was from beer my dad poured in my sippy cup. By thirteen, I had developed a real taste for it, and devised ways of getting it on my own.

@JoshD *You mention your father early on, but not later. Is he still part of the family and, if so, how have you come to terms with that history?*

By the time I entered high school, I was virtual caregiver for my younger siblings—and for my mom, who was a severely battered wife. It was during this time that I learned the reason my mother had been incapable of protecting me in childhood. Her strange moods and unexplained absences were actually symptoms of serious mental illness. She was diagnosed with chronic depression, obsessive-compulsive disorder, and Multiple Personality Disorder. It was her intense and unwavering faith in God that gave her solace and the strength to endure during those critical times. Even at her weakest points in life, she clung to her convictions and used all of the energy she could muster to give each of her children a solid Bible education. She remains a shining example of what a Christian woman should be. Although my life has not followed her exact spiritual path, she gave me a religious foundation, and her fighting spirit to survive is a constant inspiration to me.

After nearly twenty-five years of struggle, for the most part I've overcome my own personal demons. Still, a voice from childhood, a negative one, occasionally speaks to me. It asserts that I'm not good enough, or smart enough, or pretty enough. It tells me that I'm not accepted for who I am inside, but rather labeled by

@JoshD *Those negative voices are tough to fight and affect everything from interpersonal relationships to financial planning to career growth.*

the differences that define me. It pushes my mind to the times kids scoffed when I explained I didn't celebrate Christmas or birthdays. I pretended not to care. When I wouldn't join in with the bad words, the kids sneered behind my back. I ignored that, too. I refused to pledge allegiance or salute the flag. I viewed both of these acts as idol worship. When I was singled out and ridiculed by my teachers, I pretended it didn't matter, that it didn't hurt.

I recall instances when teachers, people I looked to for guidance and instruction, allowed their personal feelings and opinions to overshadow their sense of fairness when my religious beliefs differed from their own. There were teachers who were so obviously disapproving of my religion that it affected their interactions with me, and sometimes even my grades.

These experiences and many others left me feeling ashamed and silent, hiding in a covert life of drugs and alcohol. I couldn't explain any of these things then, but I could write about them. And writing, at an early age, became the lifeline that anchored me to my sanity.

And then one day, on a day like any other, as I careened along my course of self-destruction, a caring teacher, Dr. Toni Walters, unknowingly snatched me from that path by assigning a simple writing project. As usual, I was high. But my brain managed to work, and my fingers eventually flew at the notebook on the desk in front of me, and when my pen came to rest, emotions that I never knew I had had spilled forth onto my paper.

"Cry" is a poem that emerged from those dark days.

Cry

Angry
words
stream
from
fingertips
staining
paper
with
words
that
never
dry
like
tears
would
stain
my
face
if
only
I
could
cry.

Erika Roman Saint-Pierre, age 14

Suddenly, I realized that I loved to write. It was freeing for me, a form of release. I've been writing ever since. It was the assignment that literally changed the course of my life; the genesis of brighter days.

Mine was a difficult adolescence, but there were many long-term—even lifetime—friendships formed during my school years with kids who befriended me and accepted our differences. There were also unexpected and, more often than not, unsolicited bright-spots—in the guise of people who saw my plight, recognized that there was injury, and wanted to help. These selfless souls assisted in saving my life. In their honor, I've embarked on a course that involves promoting culture, diversity, and literary arts education.

Memories of a painful past, and of the random acts of kindness that I experienced there, serve to fuel my passion for the work I have chosen to do today. Knowing first hand that even small things can make a difference in the life of a troubled child encourages me. It's what daily renews my mission and led to the birth of Culturatti Kids.

Culturatti Kids, a youth-based literary arts initiative, was founded on the premise that creative writing is one of the most important forms of self-expression accessible to the human spirit. We are defined by our thoughts, and our ability to express those thoughts in a precise and intelligible way is what enables us to connect with our inner selves, our peers, our environment, and with our world.

It is one of those fundamental things that sets us apart from animals, and tends to define our humanity. The ability and freedom to write is a gift that I believe should be nourished and embraced, because, like music and visual art, it's a phenomenon through which we invite ourselves, and allow others, to peer into our souls. At a very young age, children can and should be taught to respect the power and beauty of the written word. They need to see its importance as a tool for displaying their worth and the merit of the things they have to say to the world.

In many walks of life, it's vital to develop a vivid and strong sense of imagination. Creative writing encourages children to think outside of the box and leads to the development of problem-solving skills. And being good writers and avid readers helps children (and adults) to practice good grammar and to improve their spelling skills. These are facets of education that can lead to better and more gainful employment in later life.

Educators realize the importance of encouraging children and young adults to tell stories, journal, and express themselves, expanding their imaginations by means of the written word. A creative child, even one who is introverted and reluctant to verbalize his or her ideas, could grow up to be the next great journalist or novelist. Creative writing allows children to remain detached while expressing whatever is bothering them in some other voice. These are goals I would like to set before every child who expresses a love of reading and writing.

It's often difficult for children to focus and discipline themselves. When we are able to let our imaginations roam free we're actually encouraging the centering of our minds. When we place the thoughts that live inside our heads onto paper, making them something viable and pleasing for others, it is an exercise in discipline. We're teaching ourselves to become organized, clear, and succinct.

Troubled kids, those who live in poverty and disillusionment, are at greater risk. Most of these kids will not grow up to be the next great athletes, rappers, or singers. Many will fall prey to drugs or alcohol, or end up trapped within the revolving doors of the penal system. Some will fall victim to mental illness, or will remain in the dismal existence of lives lacking hope and options. But when children learn to express themselves, they free their minds and open doors.

No matter what their economic background, religion, or race, each child should know that he or she has a voice that is vital, valued, and needs to be heard. There should be a certain sense of entitlement for each one of us: knowledge that we must be treated fairly, respected for our worth, and listened to when we speak—whether that speech is verbal or on the written page. We all need to know that our thoughts, feelings, and beliefs count. There is power in words, and our becoming adept in the use of them avails us of that power. When this knowledge is reinforced in us, each of our spirits can soar in search of its place in this world.

These days, I'm blessed to be able to write children's books, visit schools, and share my story with young people. We have open discussions on race, religion, and literature. I'm constantly amazed at the way their eager young minds work. I speak to them about setting goals and following their dreams. It's rewarding work that has allowed me to live a life I would have never thought possible. I've given myself permission to excel and I try to show children that they can achieve their goals— that they can excel, too.

My first children's book, *Hoppa's Big Move,* is based on experiences that in many ways profoundly shaped the way I saw myself as a child. In order to be palatable to children, those experiences have been somewhat sanitized. But lessons I learned about bias and prejudice are examined in the book because, for now, bigotry and religious discrimination still exist.

> A man told his grandson: "A terrible fight is going on inside me—a fight between two wolves. One is evil, and represents hate, anger, arrogance, intolerance, and superiority. The other is good, and represents joy, peace, love, tolerance, understanding, humility, kindness, empathy, generosity, and compassion. This same fight is going on inside you, inside every other person too."
> The grandson then asked: "Which wolf will win?"
> The old man replied simply: "The one you feed."

This well-known parable illustrates a persistent truth. Intolerance—as well as tolerance—has to be fed and nourished. Young minds are hungry and want to be fed. We decide which qualities to feed in them. None of us is born with prejudices. These have to be taught, but once the lessons are ingrained, the legacies of intolerance endure. Children who experience the sting of prejudice can be scarred well into adulthood, and those who are on the giving end can grow up never knowing the inappropriateness of their actions.

Racial and religious intolerance divides people and can lead to conflict among individuals and nations. I've never been political. I just believe, whole-heartedly, that people are people and should be able to work out their differences through dialogue. Literature can be a unifying force that transcends racial or religious barriers. Reading thoughts and ideas different than our own educates us and fosters understanding, which can lead to tolerance and peace.

The principle of treating others the way we want to be treated is taught in most of the major religions of the world. In Christianity it's known as "The Golden Rule." It's also taught with different wording in the Jewish faith. It's unfortunate that most religions have failed to convey the scope of this teaching to their membership. Congregations often give lip service to the tenet, but, in practice, they apply "The Golden Rule" only to fellow believers. It doesn't always extend to followers of other faiths or to those who practice no religion. When we consider others to be less important than members of our own faith, the danger is that these feelings may degenerate into apathy, active discrimination, or even religiously sanctioned violence.

@JoshD *Your faith was ridiculed in childhood. Where are you today? Maybe you've come to your own spirituality out of everything that's happened—that's probably true for all of us.*

With these thoughts in mind, Culturatti Kids celebrates diversity in all its forms, and we encourage free expression and the interchange of opinion through literature. Through the work of Culturatti Kids and organizations similar to it, maybe future generations can live in a world where difference makes a difference—but in a good way. That's the dream I have. That's the world I see.

I See

I see a place where friendships grow
and love is a song that we all know.
And heartache is a distant memory
because everyone is free.
And color is just a word describing a flower, a tree or a bird,
but never does apply to me.
That's what I see.

I see a place where love's in bloom
and everyone has room
to be just who he ought to be.
That's the world I see.

I see a world where laughing eyes and voices raised in
happy cries
are lifted toward the joyful skies.
That's what I see.

I see a place where children dream;
knowing dreams really do come true.
And hope shines as brightly as the sun that beams.
That's what I see for me and you.

It's a place where friendships grow
and love is the song we have come to know.
And heartache is a fading memory
because everyone is free.
And color is just a word describing a flower, a tree or a bird,
but never does apply to me.
No, never applies to you or me.
That's what I see.

Barbara Randall (my mom)
lyrics inspired by the children's book *Hoppa's Big Move*

●

Erika's conversation partner was Joshua Dobbs. He read Erika's essay and
sent the tweets you see in the margins. Find Josh's essay, "A War on Two
Fronts" on page 24.

Looking Around
Resource Suggestions from the Author and Editors

Culturatti Kids—www.culturattikids.net

Jacob Daddy—by Barbara Randall

Questions \ for Discussion and Contemplation

1 How do you feel "different" from others? From your family? Your friends? Your local community?

2 In your darkest moments in life, who or what has been your light? Have you ever been that light to someone else?

3 Which wolf (or wolves!) are you feeding in your life? Are the fullest wolves the ones you want to triumph?

- Difference Makes a Difference

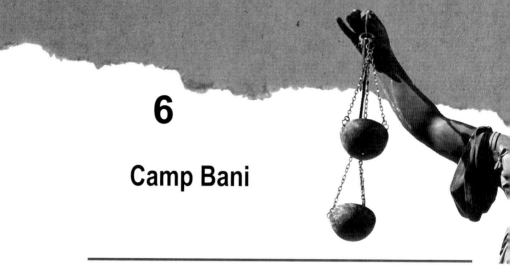

6

Camp Bani

JOE GEOGHEGAN AND CHLOE GRAMMER

Editor's Note: Joe and Chloe traveled to the Dominican Republic in July of 2009. At the time, they were recent high school graduates and this trip was their last of such trips with their church youth group. They spent a week at Camp Bani, a Methodist camp and conference center run by various local churches and the overseas mission branch of the United Methodist Church. Their hosts, to whom they often refer, were Kim and Damon Bland, Methodist missionaries. The people they highlight in this essay each deserve their own book; for now, Joe and Chloe tell their stories, hoping that doing so will lead to a greater understanding of what it means for all of us to reach out to others.

Chloe

As we approached the ladies who stood in front of the kitchen, they greeted us with warm, welcoming smiles. I have to admit, however, that I was wondering if we would even be able to get past the language barrier. Several times throughout the week it had proven to be extremely difficult to overcome. The youngest, whose name I never even learned, waved me closer. She proceeded to point at my shoes: my old, worn-out running shoes that had been around for about as long as I could remember. They were dirty, covered in paint, and probably not smelling the greatest. At first I didn't quite understand, but it didn't take long to catch on. She liked and even *wanted* my shoes! I was flattered and felt a feeling of satisfaction swell inside me. A few days before, Kim, one of our leaders, had informed us of a local program that was collecting shoes for those in need. I had planned on leaving my tennis shoes anyway, but now, even better, I got to see firsthand who they would be going to. And as quickly as I felt that joy fill my heart, my stomach dropped even quicker, draining every feeling of happiness from me. I looked at the woman's feet; they were ashen, calloused, and bare. I couldn't believe this was happening.

We had been at Camp Bani for five days, served two out of the three meals a day by this woman, and not a single one of us had realized she had had no shoes on. Of course I told her she could have them; I would find her before we left. But, as we walked away in silence I almost couldn't bear to be in my own skin. How could I have been so insensitive and selfish to think everybody has shoes? My entire life I had been wrapped in a world full of luxury, comfort, and little worry, and, up until that moment, I had never encountered a situation as real and heartbreaking as this one. Sure I had seen homeless people living on the streets, poverty-stricken communities, and towns that had been ripped apart by natural disasters, but in my mind nothing could compare to this at that moment. This was the icing on the cake that forced me to realize just how many times in our everyday lives we take for granted commodities that, while common in North America, may not necessarily be so everywhere else.

In the Dominican Republic and all over the world, things such as shoes, running water, a place to feel safe, or even a house are not conveniences for everyone possesses. Going through an entire day's work without an adequate food or water supply is something that many of us have trouble imagining. Since that day at Camp Bani, I have felt challenged and inspired to never stop being grateful for the wonderful gifts I have been blessed with, and to never allow barriers to keep me from interacting with someone, because for all I know within that person just may be something life changing.

Martin Luther King Jr. once stated, "Life's most important question is: What are you doing for others?" In a society that is too often focused on egocentric goals and achievements, a saying such as this is frequently found to be absurd. But how can this be when so many of us have grown up hearing "The

Golden Rule" and learning the importance of sharing with others, even when it is not easy? Sure, there are those who donate generous amounts to charities, and those who give weekly contributions to the church, but no sum of money compares to the gift of time and service to those in need.

My week in the Dominican Republic could not have taught me any greater lesson. Some people believe that, if they give and do not receive anything in return, they are at a loss. What these people sadly do not realize is that giving is a win-win situation! When you give of yourself and expect nothing in return, you increase your ability to love, and a sense of gratification develops. Not only that: being generous brings more happiness than self-indulgence. The feeling you get when you know you are making a difference in someone else's life is incredible and unlike any other.

@Shelvis&Nancy *So true, Chloe. Language or other barriers can keep us from connecting in a meaningful way, but we can overcome those limitations!*

Joe

We touched down under the cover of darkness, the transition from air to ground transportation our first clue that we had indeed arrived in a foreign land. We tried to overcome the language barrier to bargain down the price of having our luggage driven to the camp behind us. On the road, countryside and shanties whipped past us on each side and we got lost countless times. There was so much to see, but we could barely take time to notice it through our sleepiness and the overwhelming darkness outside. Besides, this was Latin America. Hadn't the Discovery Channel already shown us what there was outside?

Our arrival at Camp Bani was no small event, and even in the wee hours when we arrived, things were eventful. Perhaps the Discovery Channel might have glossed over a few things. In some of our housing, there was only one light bulb to be shared between two rooms of bunks and a bathroom. That first night, thirty of us plopped down into some of the worst living conditions that any of us had ever experienced.

Little did we know that this was just the first step.

Over the next week we would have to fully get over ourselves and put our pride aside to appreciate the experience that we were about to be part of.

Kim and Damon had already achieved this end. After short professional lives of their own, they now host mission trips in the Dominican Republic. Extremely kind and flexible, they host groups, camps, and even interns. Though not living in the most ideal conditions, Kim and Damon have been willing to let their lives be steered in whichever fashion seemed most right to them and right for the world. They were inspiring, to say the least.

Our first day at camp we learned that our week was not to be spent alone—a big group of Dominican teenagers was spending the same week at the campsite that we were. We had come to "do mission"; they were just coming to church camp. We had only begrudgingly accepted even the nicer facilities at the camp; they took the remaining dorms without complaint. We had donned our oldest shoes and rattiest clothes for the week; they arrived in their finest attire for a few days of fun and communion with God. We spent our days building a ten-foot-high cement wall around the camp property; they would change the way we thought and related to the world forever.

The Dominican campers held worship services every night—and we were invited to attend, but our integration was slow. Only a few of us poked our heads in on the first night; however, by the last night every single one of us was inside and on our feet for as many hours as we could handle. Sometimes faith is inspiring. Sometimes it is humbling. Sometimes it is overwhelming. These Dominican kids' services were all of the above. they all sang, danced, and yelled praise as if they had secretly been practicing Christianity their entire lives. For us North American Midwesterners, used to Protestant congregations where bringing a little life into a worship service is a constant struggle, watching these kids just like us worship was an overwhelming experience.

Even more humbling than those around us were those who were working "for" us. Despite the camp's limited funds, there were two cooks, two people helping us with the wall, and the groundskeeper Ernessimo—all employed under the camp. Each had his or her own story, every one of them more real than anything reported in our newspapers, and often more heart-wrenching than *Lolita*. One early morning I ran into Ernessimo before the rest of the camp was awake. As we began to talk, he told me about all of his family abroad in the United States. They were doctors, lawyers, and teachers. Taken aback, I finally asked Ernessimo what had kept him in this little corner of the Dominican. In his barely decipherable Spanish, Ernessimo told me that he loved it there too much, that he loved the people and was able to support some of his family who were still there. Everyone, Ernessimo explained, deserved at least to have a minimal livelihood, and his staying at Camp Bani allowed that to happen. I was speechless.

 @Shelvis&Nancy *The women serving meals and the stories of strangers who became friends remind me that the mutual gift of "serving" transforms us all.*

The most inspiring story related in our presence, however, came from a Haitian named Raoul. His family's house had been destroyed by a hurricane, there were no job opportunities in Haiti, and many of those around him had responded by falling into drugs or a bottle. Raoul was different. He moved across the border to the Dominican Republic, where today many of the country's hardest workers are Haitian immigrants. Raoul was no exception. Kim and Damon hired him for pennies per day and Raoul was as productive as any ten of us. Raoul worked on problems in a foreign country in order to solve his own problems at home.

What did all of these wonderful people that we met in the Dominican Republic—Kim, Damon, Raoul, Ernessimo—have in common? What was it that made them different, that gave them such an incredible aura? *They were people living for a purpose larger than themselves.* Be it family, friends, God, kids, or ending poverty, they had all embraced something bigger, learning along the way that life carries so much more meaning when you do.

Our week in the Dominican Republic ended with us in almost the opposite mindset than that with which we had arrived. We had entered that campground at Camp Bani wondering if we could help, if we could live under those conditions, if we could overcome a language barrier and commune with people who seemingly shared so little in common with us. We left having been changed more than we changed, wondering if we could return with a good conscience to the luxury of home, wondering if we could go to a home so far from the Dominican Republic.

@Shelvis&Nancy *Amen, Joe. Anywhere in the world, encountering people of great faith is inspiring, humbling, and overwhelming. Well said.*

On that last night, the Dominican kids were gone, and we were back together as a group. But the group had changed. There was an understanding silence as we watched the sun go down from the roof of the kitchen. The mountains were too beautiful, too untouched. The serenity and the new-world charm than emanated from this entire island was a double-edged sword. The dirt roads and quaint villages were much more a representation of people struggling to get by than a utopia of people having returned to nature. As we reflected on all that we had learned, all that we had gained from our trip, I could not help but think what real gains seem to come when you don't make it all about you.

●

● Joe and Chloe's conversation partners were Shelvis and Nancy Smith-Mather. They read Joe and Chloe's essay and sent the tweets you see in the margins. Find Shelvis and Nancy's essay, "Reflections from East Africa," on page 13.

Looking Around
Resource Suggestions from the Author and Editors

Dominican Republic Missions Project
http://dominicanrepublicmissions.com/youth.aspx

Questions \for Discussion and \Contemplation

1 What are some barriers you can think of that we humans build between ourselves? Are they of our own imagining and choosing, or are they real, valid, something to truly be grappled with?

2 Are you living your life in a way that acknowledges something bigger at work? If not, how could you?

3 Think about a time in your life when you had a barrier to overcome between you and another person (it may even be one of the barriers you listed in question one). How did you overcome it?

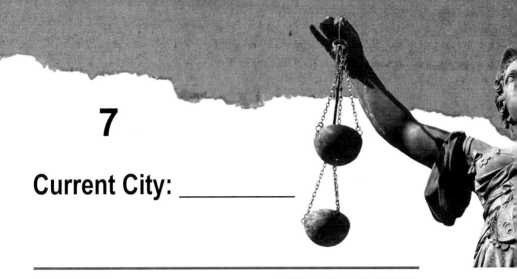

7

Current City: _____

My current city listing on Facebook of Juba, Sudan, indicates my life isn't quite "normal." Perhaps even more puzzling would have been my previous "city" listing of Méguet, Burkina Faso. I was forced by Facebook to list the village of Méguet as a city, when in reality it is very much indicative of the way of life in rural West Africa. It's all bucket baths underneath constellations of stars, laborious subsistence farming, and, thankfully, rich communal living, which helps one forget that Burkina Faso is one of the least developed nations in West Africa.

Facebook also reminds me from where I have come. Most of my friends have Lancaster, Pennslyvania, or Indianapolis, Indiana, or somewhere within a relatively short drive of these locales, listed as their current city—and this makes sense. I attended an affluent, suburban high school in Lancaster, and continued with my studies at Manchester College, a liberal arts college surrounded by the corn and soy fields of northern Indiana.

I am still perplexed as to why I enrolled at Manchester. After all, I used to become homesick shortly after the departure of my parents from the overnight soccer camps that I attended as a teenager. Surely, attending college 600 miles from home should have been ruled out of the question. If I had followed own precedent after completing high school, I would have ventured to State College, Pa., and spent most of my fall afternoons cheering on my beloved Nittany Lions with 110,000 raucous blue and white supporters, screaming, "WE ARE...*PENN STATE!*" at the top of our lungs. In retrospect, I'm thankful that I instead followed the Pennsylvania Turnpike west to West Virginia and through Ohio, before ultimately arriving in Wabash County, Indiana.

The majority of my class work at Manchester was confined to the third floor of the administration building, where the accounting and business department is located. However, most of the learning that inspired my interest in global affairs and, in particular, Sub-Saharan Africa, occurred elsewhere. The classroom I truly enjoyed was rather impromptu, and as time progressed, this classroom expanded from the third floor of the administration building to the not-so-traditional academic venue of the soccer training grounds, where I trained with teammates that hailed from Ghana, Nigeria, and Liberia. In addition to the soccer pitch, my off-campus apartment, where I shared countless meals and cups of tea and coffee with students coming from all corners of the globe, became a forum for discussions concerning international affairs that habitually lasted well into the early morning.

I was oblivious to the profound impact that these friendships would have on my worldview, especially in the post-9/11 era. As the horrific events of that Tuesday morning unfolded, and certain American media outlets were quick to demonize practitioners of Islam, I was quick to realize that these declarations were drastically off base. Ultimately, the events of September 11, 2001, would change my 2002 January session plans as the repercussions reverberated, not only in the United States, but also in Nigeria, where I had hoped to take a cultural anthropology class. Instead of travelling to Abuja, Nigeria, I found myself in sunny Jamaica (though not the Jamaica that I had experienced beforehand aboard a cruise ship). Instead of spending one day in Negril before continuing to the next port-of-call, I spent a month shuttling between urban centers and rural milieus. While I witnessed rural poverty and the disparities that exist between the urban rich and poor, which are ever so present in the developing world, I also observed moments of transformation that an outsider does not usually associate with life in developing countries. Perhaps most inspiring was the work of Kenneth Wilson, who single-handedly united groups of politically divided youth through the use of soccer, and, by doing so, transformed August Town, a historically tumultuous section of Kingston, where escalating political tensions once had the tendency to outpace the daily increase in temperature, into a peaceful working-class quarter. Not only did this month serve as my introduction to community rehabilitation and development work in the global south, it also forced me to profoundly reconsider the reasons behind my pursuit of my degree in accounting and management, which had up until that point centered strictly upon me.

After returning from Jamaica, it became increasingly difficult to turn a blind eye to the developing world. Previously I had been able to change the channel when the news reports coming from certain regions became burdensome, effectively ignoring the voices emanating from these locales. But after having personally witnessed similar daily struggles, these accounts began to profoundly resonate with me. I could no longer content myself by merely exploring the issues of the global south from the comfortable environs of the United States.

Over the course of the next several years, I had the opportunity to study International Relations and African History, both well outside of the scope of my requisite accounting and management classes. These classes, combined with two friendships in particular—the first, with a student who had fled the violence of the Second Sudanese Civil War; and the second, with a student who had been displaced from Uganda during the reign of terror perpetrated by Idi Amin, and as a result was forced to seek refuge in South Africa—further increased my interest in African affairs. Looking back, these reasons alone demonstrate the ignorance with which I viewed the African continent at this period of my life. I was very much in tune with the "Hollywood" version of Africa, and my ever-expanding collection of DVDs attested to this fact. Furthermore, as the genocide in Darfur, Western Sudan, escalated, and became an American *cause celebre,* my attention once again shifted back to Sub-Saharan Africa, but again in a superficial manner. While this phase of my life, without doubt, laid the foundation for my current undertakings, it would be another two years before I would finally have the opportunity to set foot on the African continent.

After working as an insurance auditor for what was quickly approaching two years, waking up in the morning and going to the office became a tedious chore. While it was nice to have a regular salary, and, as I would learn starting in October 2007, a luxury, it was evident that a change in career focus was necessary. As the adage goes, "Money can't buy happiness," and while I had heard this stated countless times, it wasn't until this point of my life that I fully comprehended its meaning. I was being tugged emotionally in what seemed like a million different directions. The perfect remedy for this situation was a weekend in North Manchester with Felix Lohitai, my friend from college, who was quickly becoming my advisor on all issues African. That weekend, over endless cups of tea, we discussed the various ways in which I could make my escape to the African continent, the same continent that he had been forced to flee twenty years earlier. By the time that I left North Manchester that Sunday afternoon, I had decided to join the United States Peace Corps.

@Kendra *To be a catalyst for change and justice, we must move from "student," seeking knowledge and understanding, to "practitioner," learning and living alongside others.*

That was the easy part. For the next two weeks, I grappled with how I would inform my family. I was convinced that they would think that I was out of my mind. I began envisioning all of the possible questions that they would pose, as well as my probable responses. Finally, I broke my silence, and to my surprise my family was 100 percent supportive. Perhaps I should have expected such a reaction, given my family's lineage in the Church of the Brethren, one of the historic peace churches and a proponent of pursuing social justice issues domestically and abroad. At the time of my departure for Philadelphia, my mother quoted Mahatma Gandhi: "You must be the change you wish to see in the world." I suspect, though, that she probably thought that upon setting foot in Burkina Faso and encountering the reality of life in the Sahel, I would quickly return to the States.

Admittedly, I did constantly wonder if I was making a mistake by leaving a source of steady income—along with all of the other luxuries that we, as Americans, take for granted—for an employment opportunity that would pay me roughly ten dollars per day in one of the least developed countries in the world. I knew that Burkina Faso was "poor" before arriving in Ouagadougou, the capital. Its ranking on the United Nations Human Development Index, which holistically measures the development level of a given country, ranks "The Land of Honest Men" as the third least-developed country in the world. Furthermore, Mali and Niger, two countries which border Burkina, rank 178 and 182 respectively on the development index, making this region of West Africa one of its most impoverished. Attempting to understand these statistics before having set foot in Burkina proved impossible. However, it did prompt further questions: What would it be like to be a relatively affluent American living in a rural African village? What did such deprivation look like? Perhaps the only certainty was that I was en route to receive a crash course in living simply, relationship building, and service. Although these are perhaps the three Church of the Brethren teachings that had resonated most with me prior to my departure, the twenty-seven months that I lived in Burkina Faso exponentially increased my understanding of these core values.

On October 7, 2007, as Air France flight number 732 started its descent into Ouagadougou, I was afforded my first glimpse of the Sahel. Descending from the north, after traversing the southernmost expanse of the Sahara Desert, the approach into Ouagadougou is checkered with earthen-red colored villages until arriving at the city limits, at which time the corrugated metal roofing and reflecting Sahelian sunlight provide a blinding affect to those perched slightly below the cloud line. Upon landing, in synchronization with the opening of the hatch, the rolling heat that signifies your arrival in the Sahel engulfs the cabin of the plane, as if this act has been rehearsed countless times. Two days later I would encounter rural Burkina Faso, this time from the confines of a scorching hot bus as I ventured 180 kilometers north to Ouahigouya, a regional capital near the border with Mali in northwest Burkina Faso.

Current City: _____

63

At this moment, Burkina seemed anything but the exotic land that I had envisioned while I was still stateside. It was a poverty-stricken, oppressively hot, arid country. As I passed in and out of sleep on this searing hot journey, I was oblivious as to how my initial impression of Burkina would start to change two days later.

October 10, 2007, was the day that I became a member of *la famille Ganamé* and started to develop a bond that I hope will not be breached regardless of my proximity or lack thereof to Ouahigouya. While I am blessed to consider the Ganamés part of my family, the process of building this relationship was not without some tribulation. Those theories about relationships taking a living form and needing to be constantly nourished had never resonated so clearly in my life. While the first night was quite an adventure, which tested the uppermost limit of my comfort zone, it became apparent rather quickly that we as a family were in this for the long run, and that the Ganamés would do everything in their power to nurture my growth as a person while at the same time fostering my comprehension of Burkinabé societal norms. This togetherness eased the culture shock that I encountered upon leaving the United States for Burkina Faso and provided me with what I needed most at that time—a family that would fill the void that had up until my departure been filled by my friends and family in the States. Togetherness would become a recurrent theme throughout the time I would spend in Burkina.

Ten weeks later, I would leave the comforting surroundings of the Ganamé house and once again attempt to resume my life, this time in the village of Méguet, twenty-five miles from a paved road and without modern amenities such as running water and electricity. The next two years of my life would force me to grow as a global citizen, as well as challenge me to develop creative solutions to address some of the problems in one of the most destitute countries in the world. Moreover, I would be challenged on a daily basis to live simply, peacefully, and as part of a village where I was the only westerner amongst 5,400 habitants.

Luckily, as had been the case during my time in Ouahigouya, I would soon be accepted as a member in another family. The Soudrés became to me what the Ganamés had been during my initial three months in Burkina Faso. Food and conversation were constantly available and, in stark contrast to customs in the U.S., no prior arrangements announcing that I was coming were necessary. Such is the way of life in Sub-Saharan Africa. Here one is truly blessed to have an extended network of family and friends, and, as an American, being considered part of this family and no longer seen as a "Nasarra," or foreigner, was truly a blessing.

@Kendra *What constitutes home? How do we enter someone else's? How can we work for justice in a community we weren't born into? How do we return to the home of our birth to work for justice?*

As time passed, I started to become more and more disconnected from the life that I had once led in the United States. Those bucket baths under the stars that once seemed like such a foreign concept became the norm, as well as living without electricity. The poverty, which had once been omnipresent, began to fade into the plateau-laden landscape that characterizes central Burkina Faso, and what had appeared as sufferance at the time of my arrival had given way to joy and inspiration.

As my service progressed, I witnessed on a first-hand basis the impediments to development that poorly financed education and healthcare delivery systems play in developing countries. It is not uncommon for an underpaid teacher to have more than one hundred students in his or her classroom, the majority of whom come to school on a daily basis without having eaten a nutritious meal—an imperative for cognitive development. The overall literacy rate of Burkina Faso, which stands at 28.7 percent, directly reflects these impediments. Living in Méguet also afforded me the opportunity to acquire experience in malaria and HIV/AIDS prevention, in addition to working with women's groups on issues related to child nutrition.

However, beyond the opportunities to interact with the local community on small-scale development projects, the memories that I cherish pertain to the personal relationships that I developed with my neighbors. By sharing meals with numerous families on a regular basis, learning to speak the local language—Moore—toiling behind a plow drawn by a donkey, and celebrating both traditional holidays and special occasions (such as weddings and baptisms), I was able to fully integrate into the village of Méguet society and gain a deep appreciation for the way of life in central Burkina Faso. These images will rest forever in the back of my mind and will definitely serve as a source of motivation for creating the change that not only I, but the populations that I serve, hope to see.

The change in my current Facebook location to Juba, Southern Sudan, signifies that a new adventure in my life has begun. While there are numerous inherent challenges associated with working for a grassroots development organization in a post-conflict country, the satisfaction that is derived when a new school is constructed, which will allow school-aged children to gain an education that would not have been possible otherwise, is truly rewarding. The world knows all too well that Sudan has been embroiled in internal conflicts for thirty-nine of the past fifty years. These conflicts have resulted in the deaths of more than 2 million persons and have forced countless others from their homeland as refugees.

As a result of these conflicts, development efforts have been limited primarily to the provincial capitals. The disparity in development between Southern Sudan and even Burkina Faso is astonishing. While Burkina Faso is extremely underdeveloped, especially in the rural communes such as Méguet, the Burkinabé transportation system does a remarkable job of connecting these communities with the regional capitals. Such a system is nonexistent in Southern Sudan, which hinders even the most mundane tasks, resulting in communities that have been deprived of health and education infrastructure as well as opportunities for economic advancement. The Burkinabe Federal

@Kendra *International development is wrought with many inequities. What is the role of justice and equity in existing models of international development?*

Government, despite its limited resources, has also done a remarkable job in decentralizing public services. As a result, in most Burkinabé villages inhabitants are able to access essential health treatment when needed. This is once again in stark contrast to the situation in Southern Sudan. While I am no longer in Burkina, there is rarely a day that passes without me reminiscing about the time that I lived in Méguet. These mental images are the driving forces that enliven me when I feel as if my energy has been sapped. Burkina Faso has prepared me to be of service in Sudan, and I wholeheartedly believe that my experiences in Sudan will prepare me for the next chapter of my life. If nothing else, I will have a new collection of names and faces to spur me on in my effort to serve as a catalyst for change.

●

● Michael's conversation partner was Kendra Dunbar. She read Mike's essay and sent the tweets you see in the margins. Find Kendra's essay, "Legacy, Responsibility, and Faith" on page 32.

Questions \ for Discussion and Contemplation

1 Have you ever changed the course of your life so dramatically that it led you to question who you are, or where you are, or who you want to be? What was that like?

2 What does "family" mean to you? Who do you call family?

3 How can you be a catalyst for change in your own community?

8

And Let's Be Honest...

JOSHUA E. PERRY

Dear Professor Perry:

I hope you're doing well and enjoying the fall in Bloomington. It's hard to believe that I've been out of law school for over a year now! If you wouldn't mind, I'd like to seek your advice on something.

After graduation and the bar exam, I joined the Real Estate group at my law firm here in Seattle. I'm happy to have a job, and getting paid is much better than living on school loans, but the issue is (and here's where I'm hoping you might be able to offer some advice) I feel extremely unsatisfied and restless in my job. I'm not sure if I feel this way because I've had a hard time accepting the red tape and hierarchy and focus on money and billable hours that comes with practicing at a private law firm, or if it's simply because I'm just not meant to be a lawyer. Now that I come to think about it, I only decided to be a lawyer because my parents and teachers encouraged me to go in this direction.

At this point, I think I need a little perspective, and I thought of you because I remembered that you seemed to have faced similar challenges after law school. If you don't mind my asking, when did you know that the practice of law wasn't right for you? How much time did you give yourself to determine what you wanted to do next and how did you sort all of this out?

I apologize if this appears to be completely out of the blue. I just thought that if there were anyone that might understand some of my concerns, it would be you! I hope you and your family are doing well, and life is good.

Warm regards,

Ryan

So the title of this book claims that "it" is not all about you. And of course if by "it" we mean life—more specifically what you do with *your* life—then that is absolutely correct, as so many authors in this book have provocatively and persuasively illustrated. Your life is absolutely not all about you. But "it" does *begin* with you and your commitment to the process of discovering what Frederick Buechner describes as the work where "your deep gladness" meets the world's "deep hunger." If you are serious about wanting your life to be about serving others, saving the environment, giving back to your community, or otherwise leaving the world a little better place than you found it, well then, your life's work must begin with you discovering *you,* who *you*

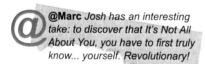

@Marc *Josh has an interesting take: to discover that It's Not All About You, you have to first truly know... yourself. Revolutionary!*

are, what lights *you* up, and what specific gifts *you* have been given. You've got to be self-educated about what brings *you* deep gladness.

If you buy the premise of this book that it's not all about you, but rather about investing your time and talents in work that has purpose and meaning beyond you and your own sense of fulfillment and well-being, you will, paradoxically perhaps, have to first do some essential work that can only begin with you. You will have to take seriously what Parker Palmer calls "the work before the work"—the inner journey of reflection and introspection that leads to self-awareness.

I guess if we're just talking about a random Saturday morning spent cleaning-up an inner-city park, a December evening spent caroling in a retirement center, or a one-off Spring Break mission trip spent giving aid in some far-flung developing nation, then the process of personal preparation and introspective self-discovery I have in mind might not be completely necessary. Any of us can show up and be present for a short-term act of random kindness.

But I'm talking about a much deeper and more profound commitment: a life that integrates "doing good for others" or "serving God" or "making the world a better place" with how you earn your living, why you get out of bed in the morning, and what you think about throughout the day. I am talking about finding what Buddhists refer to as "right livelihood," or a way of supporting yourself that nourishes your commitment to being an agent of love and compassion who lives each day in a way that reduces some amount of suffering in the world. The process of self-discovery I'm talking about is required if you want to live your days with this deep and integrated commitment to others, because, without an authentic awareness of "this is who I am and this is what I am supposed to be doing," you are not going to be much good for very long to anyone, including yourself.

Dear Ryan:

Over the years that I've been teaching I have received a number of e-mails very similar to yours, and, as I've said to my former law students in the past, I'll be the first to buy you a beer to celebrate your courage to be honest with yourself about the awareness that something about your current situation isn't the right fit for you. Just to be abundantly clear—you are not alone with these feelings, and, if it needs to be stated explicitly, you are not a "failure" or "disappointment" for considering alternative careers besides practicing real estate law in Seattle. I recall vividly the reaction of a junior partner at my law firm with about ten years of experience, who, on my last day, confided in me that he wished he had had the courage eight years earlier to discover and pursue his passions, but now it was too late because of financial obligations and missed opportunities. He said now he was trapped. And he had a tear in his eye.

To briefly answer your questions, I guess sort of like you I began having feelings of restlessness similar to what you describe after about two years of law practice. I knew I needed to escape the relentless minutiae of the practice that was slowly killing my soul (not to be too dramatic about it). Plus, my first child Ivy had just been born, and I was freaked out about the future reality of having to tell her one day that the reason Daddy missed so much of her childhood was because he was basically working 60–70 hours a week so he might one day make partner.

Initially, I didn't know whether I wanted to try to change the scenery by moving to a larger firm in a different part of the country or whether I wanted to leave the practice of law entirely—a scary proposition for many reasons. During this time of psychological upheaval, I was fortunate to discover a book that helped clarify much of my angst and confusion, and I've recommended it to a ton of people over the years. I still go back and reread it on occasion. Callings: Finding and Following an Authentic Life *by Gregg Levoy really is a profoundly insightful and eye-opening book (and it's beautifully written). Later, I would discover Parker Palmer, whose book* A Hidden Wholeness *has also been enormously helpful to me and many of my students. Palmer is a sage.*

Reading Levoy's book about listening to and responding to our life's callings, I began to realize and remember a lot of things about myself, including my interests and strengths and passions. I gained clarity on what I had to offer the world. I realized that being a lawyer, despite the good that I could do for many people and also for society, was not an authentic identity for me that resonated in a way that prompted "deep gladness." After a long process of many months, I began to realize that academia was really where I belonged. I realized that the authentic place for me to best contribute life and love to the world was in an environment where I could teach and write and work with big ideas, students, and similarly committed colleagues. Through the process of doing the work before the work, i.e., personal reflection and introspection, it became clear to me that the responsibilities and lifestyle of a college professor would feed my soul in ways that would allow me to feed the souls of other people and give back to the world in a variety of ways. And as I had anticipated, most of my days as a professor begin and end with me feeling fulfilled, empowered, and proud of how I spend my time and

@Marc Josh turned down the path of prestige and $$$ as an attorney for a life as an educator—seems he helped others and himself in the process.

talents. In other words, my life is definitely not all about me, but it certainly begins there.

But back to you, Ryan. It sounds to me like your unsettled feelings are prompting you to begin "the work before the work." A journey to that place where you can give back to the world and others begins right where you are now: asking hard, honest, and complicated questions that require reflective and introspective consideration about who you are, what's most important to you, and what you're best at: i.e., what skills, training, and talents you have to offer the world.

A final word: For me this process (and it is a process that in some ways never really ends) of transition away from the life of a lawyer and into the life of an academic was not always easy. Certainly there were those who initially questioned what appeared to some as an abrupt and unwise life change. Even after I tried to explain my rationale, not everybody always understood (not my law partners, not my parents) why I was asking so many "dangerous" questions and leaving so much potential in the law behind me. And, frankly, my career move did not make much financial sense at the time. But these questions that I was asking (and you are now asking) are THE most important questions, and they are questions that illuminate a process of personal discovery that I wholeheartedly encourage you to begin living into. Go read Levoy and Palmer. And there are others out there who can support your journey inward. Whoever you consult directly during this process, be open to receiving clues from unusual or unexpected guides. You never know where insights or inspiration might be lurking.

Anyway, those are just a few of my random thoughts. Again, I'm really glad you reached out to me and shared a little bit of what you're going through. I know it's not easy. Actually, I recall it being a little scary at times, but also exhilarating. I guess, as with most really important and profound situations one encounters in life, a real kaleidoscope of emotions is evoked.

And it all can be exhausting and overwhelming some days, so please remember to be extra kind and caring to yourself as you are going through all this soul-searching stuff and make time to exercise, drink plenty of water, breathe, etc.

Keep me in the loop and let me know if I can be of any additional help. And let me know if you're passing through Bloomington so I can buy you that celebratory beer. Just getting onto this path of self-discovery is an enormous success.

Kindest regards,

Josh

Contemplate your current situation, whether you are working, going to school, or riding trains around Europe, and ask yourself this: Can I be an agent for good in the world if I am personally not in a good spiritual or emotional place? If I am frustrated and burned-out and going through the motions just to get a paycheck or just to get a grade or just to make it through the day, am I really bringing a life-giving energy of love and compassion to those people I encounter and the tasks I undertake? If I am personally suffering in my job or my relationship or my environment, can I, over the long term, alleviate the suffering of others?

After teaching hundreds of undergraduates, law students, medical students, and business students over the years, and staying in touch with many of them after they leave my classes, I am convinced that the answer to those questions is either "no," "not effectively," or "not for very long." In other words, you can't be much good to the world or anyone else if you yourself are not in a good place to begin with. You must first get in the habit of being quiet with yourself, listening to yourself, and being gentle with yourself. You must pay attention to and take care with this inner process of discovering what nourishes and stimulates your body, mind, and soul in ways that bring you fully to life.

A few months after my correspondence with Ryan, on a late Monday afternoon, I received four tweets from @CornelWest, the Princeton University professor who describes himself as "one of America's most provocative public intellectuals [and] a champion for racial justice through the traditions of the black Church, progressive politics, and jazz." This is what he tweeted:

CornelWest For young people, its been diff to shift from bling bling, g-string, egoism, narcissism, & hedonism to

truth, justice, compassion, & service
4:27 PM Mar 29th via web

CornelWest ...That's what education in its deepest sense is—the turning of the soul.
4:30 PM Mar 29th via web

CornelWest The aim of education is to shift people from the surface to something substantive.
4:32 PM Mar 29th via web

CornelWest You can have all the schooling in the world, but if you're still on the surface, you're not really educated.
4:33 PM Mar 29th via web

We are always at the same time both teachers and students who are both educating and being educated in a variety of venues. University lecture halls, houses of worship, the inner city, a garden, a forest, or a kitchen table—it does not really matter. Regardless of our environment, audience, co-laborers, or dining companions, the substantive self-education that Professor West describes is precisely what we must attempt to foster among those in our sphere of influence and in ourselves. This authentic "turning of the soul" toward a self-awareness that leads us deep below the surface is the enduring self-education that is necessary for any of us seeking to live a life that is not all about ourselves.

@Marc *After reading this essay, I wonder what percentage of people truly feel the "call" discussed, and how many actually pursue it...???*

And let's be honest—it can indeed be difficult at any age to shift the focus from self to service, especially when so much of the pop culture universe celebrates the self above all else. It is difficult, but not impossible. With what West labels "education in its deepest sense" or what I have called the introspective process of self-discovery and reflective awareness, it is indeed possible to turn one's soul (or, in an ongoing process, to keep turning) from the surface to something substantive. You can live a life that is not all about you. But you cannot do it for very long if you remain on the surface. You must go deep with yourself. Beneath the surface and deep in the substance of *your*

@**Marc** *What brand of celebratory beer does Josh provide his former students, and where can I sign up for one?!*

@

soul is where you will find the source of strength and inspiration to make the connections between what you have to give and what the world and those around you really need.

Josh's conversation partner was Marc Istook. He read Josh's essay and sent the tweets you see in the margins. Find Marc's essay, "Call," on page 3.

Looking Around
Resource Suggestions from the Author and Editors

Wishful Thinking: A Seeker's ABC—Frederick Buechner

Callings: Finding and Following an Authentic Life—Gregg Levoy

A Hidden Wholeness: The Journey Toward An Undivided Life—Parker Palmer

Questions \for Discussion and Contemplation

1 Where does your "deep gladness" meet the world's "deep need"?

2 What in your life is life-giving, nourishing for you? What isn't?

3 Does your life need to be shifted from "self" to "service"? What would this look like for you?

And Let's Be Honest...

9

The Day We Didn't Go to Church

AMY JONASON

It started out like any other Sunday...

Well, not quite. I was going on four years living in Grand Rapids, Michigan, and this was the worst winter I had seen yet. In fact, it was the snowiest winter on record for the city; by its end we had seen over 100 inches of the stuff. So that chilly February morning was unusually treacherous. Still, we were going to church.

"We" were my housemate, Annie, and I. It was my senior year of college, and I had moved into a 100-year-old mansion near downtown Grand Rapids to participate in a program called Project Neighborhood. Eight students from my college and a "mentor" family, consisting of a married couple and their two sons, lived in this three-story house together in intentional community while learning more about the city and volunteering in different social service ministries. Across the street from us was a group home for developmentally disabled adults. Over the past several months we had gotten to know many of that house's residents, and several stopped by regularly to visit, chat, and share the ups and downs of daily life. It was both a joy and a challenge to get to know them while also learning how to balance those relationships with our relationships with each other, friends outside of our household, and, of course, schoolwork. Six of us were graduating at the end of the semester, and academic pressures bore down forcefully on all of us.

I'm fuzzy on the nonpertinent details of that particular Sunday morning, but I can say pretty confidently that it was February, it was cold, and I was depressed. At the time that was a recent revelation. It would take over a year for me to learn that the cause of my depression was not a chemical imbalance but an undiagnosed case of sleep apnea. On that February day, I just knew that I was tired, tired all the time, and that something was seriously wrong. It took an incredible amount of effort to get out of bed every morning, and the peace and joy I usually felt when I went to church had waned considerably. I was numb. Still, I had my housemates, and that was something to be thankful for. Weekly devotions in which we were all encouraged to share what we were going through made it impossible for me to hide my situation. I was learning to be vulnerable, to ask for help, and to lean on others for emotional support.

Annie and I bundled ourselves up by the back door. We were among the last to leave that day, since the service we were planning on attending started at 10:30 a.m. The family we lived with—Jeffrey, Lisa, and their boys—was getting ready for church service, too. I could hear Willem, age seven, and Xander, age five, running around. They were probably trying to bargain with their father for extra time on the computer later that day.

We pushed on the industrial-style bar across the back door and walked into the small parking lot. First built by a beer baron in the early 1900s, the house we called *Koinonia* became a college shortly after that, and then a boys' home, before being given to our college and turned into a community house in 1998. It still bore remnants of its past lives, with its enclosed staircases, linoleum floors, and, thankfully, multi-shower bathrooms. There was also the luxury of a parking lot in the back for our household of twelve to keep its seven cars.

It was Annie's car we headed to this time around. My car had suffered a fateful blow a couple of weeks earlier when my windshield wipers had frozen to the windshield in the "on" position. The motor was now shot, and I wasn't about to risk getting caught in a snowstorm with no working wipers. Of all of us, Annie probably used her car the least. She was committed to taking the bus to and from campus every day, and shared her car with her brother when he came to visit.

As we shivered in the cold, Annie stuck her key in the driver's side door. She tried to turn it once, and then again. "It's stuck."

"Maybe the cold froze the lock," I suggested.

"Yeah." She gave the key one more tug…and we watched in horror as the metal key bent on itself in a slow spiral. She pulled it out of the lock, hopelessly twisted. "Ohhh, shoot."

"Shoot!" I echoed. This was the latest in a string of car-related incidents that would have been comical if they hadn't been so stressful. Multiple times already that winter, we had pushed John's car to safety when it stalled in the alley, sorely in need of a new alternator. Then the windshield wipers busted on my car—only a moderately expensive repair, but still one for which no college student wants to write a check. After sleeping under a 6-inch snow blanket for several days, my car's battery died, not long after Erin's car battery drained as well. Soon after that, Erin replaced her alternator by herself, only for her driver's side mirror to reach its fateful end thanks to a six-foot icicle that dislodged itself from the roof outside of our bathroom window and plunged downward onto her parked car. It wasn't a good winter to own a car; it just wasn't a good winter to be in Grand Rapids. The snow and the ice, combined with the winter's usual string of overcast days and our unusual rash of car problems, made it seem like God had some serious beef with our part of the world.

Annie and I trudged back into the house and related what had happened to Jeffrey and Lisa. "Come to church with us," they suggested. We were cold, tired, and more determined than ever to get out of the house, so that seemed like the best option. We headed out to the van with Lisa, the boys, and Harriett. Harriett was from Uganda, and had come into town for an international development conference at the beginning of the month. She had stayed with us for a few weeks after that while she looked for more permanent work in West Michigan. She thought Grand Rapids was cold. Jeffrey found her a Calvin College jacket early on in her stay, and she had taken to wearing it everywhere, including indoors. I could hardly blame her.

The seven of us settled in—Annie, Harriet, and Xander in the back, and Willem and I in the middle seat. Lisa sat up front. Jeffrey climbed in the driver's side, started the car, and started backing slowly out of the parking lot. It had been cleared recently, but the ground was still icy.

As we angled for the driveway, we hit the first snag. A huge tree in the curve of the driveway made for a tight corner, and weeks of snowplowing had built the snow piles on either side of the driveway into three-foot drifts. Trying to look in the rearview mirror over the heads of six passengers, Jeffrey backed up and ran the car squarely into one of the drifts. He shifted forward, and we heard the tires spinning. We were stuck.

I knew that if there was one thing mild-mannered Jeffrey really hated, it was being late. The addition of extra passengers to the morning "train" had already slowed things down, and the clock was ticking toward 10:30. He hopped out of the car to assess the situation, and Lisa slid over into the driver's seat. The rest of us were stuffed in the back like clowns, full-grown adults occupying child-size bench seats in our heavy winter jackets. In the interest of time, we could do little else than watch. Jeffrey motioned to give Lisa some instructions, so she hit the button to roll down the driver's side window. "Zzt," it sputtered. It was so cold, the automatic windows weren't even working. Lisa sighed and opened the door.

"I'm going to push, and when I say 'drive,' you go forward," Jeffrey instructed. He started pushing on the front of the car to try to rock it out of its position. Push, push, push. The rest of us assisted as much as we could, leaning forward and back with the rhythm. Out of the corner of my eye I saw someone come around from behind the van. It was our neighbor, Rick. The situation was getting tenser, but good-natured Rick didn't seem to notice. He enthusiastically braced himself against the side of the van and assisted Jeffrey's efforts.

To everyone's relief, the van started to move. "Okay, drive!" Jeffrey called as he stepped to the side. Lisa put the car in drive and stepped lightly on the gas. The van rolled forward.

"Okay, now back up!" Jeffrey hollered. The driver's side door was open, but he was near the car's front bumper, and his voice sounded tinny and small through the glass of the windshield. Lisa put the car in reverse. I breathed a sigh of relief. We were gonna make it. The van began to glide backward, and then…

"WATCH THE DOOR!" I heard Jeffrey shout. It was like telling secrets underwater. His voice sounded so excited, yet so far away…Before any of us realized what was happening, the open driver's side door caught on the edge of that blasted snow bank and bent back on itself with a slow, agonizing groan. The car came to a stop.

What happened next was even more surprising. "SHIT!!!!" Jeffrey yelled. He slammed both hands down on the front of the car, glaring down at the windshield wipers and shaking his head. Then he straightened up abruptly and walked away. We watched him walk down to the corner and pace back and forth, looking up at the sky.

The mood inside the car was still. In six months of life together I had never seen Jeffrey angry, much less heard him swear. For a brief moment I was a seven-year-old kid again, watching my parents argue and feeling paralyzed with fear. I looked at the back of Lisa's head, but I couldn't tell what she was thinking. We sat in silence. And then…

"Well," Willem said matter-of-factly. "I don't think we're going to church!"

He didn't sound too upset about this. In a flash, the winter's entire chain of mishaps unfolded in my mind in all its irony, and I couldn't help it. I started giggling. This was the culmination of ridiculous. I half expected the earth to yawn beneath us and quietly engulf everyone, van, snowbank, and all.

@**Kristen** *One of the coolest things about God is how we usually experience God's presence in the moments when we do/say something "un-Christian."*

"Shh! It's not funny!" Annie whispered. She was my "older sister," trying to admonish my socially incorrect behavior before anyone noticed. I stopped laughing, but grinned to myself. My heart felt a little lighter. Things were going to be fine.

And fine they were, not too long after that. We skipped church. We trudged inside. Annie, Harriett, and I snuggled under blankets on the couch and read some devotions. Lisa and Jeffrey quickly reconciled, and called the auto-body repair shop. Later that day, Harriett flew home to Uganda. I still have a picture that we took that day before she left, several of us all sitting together on the couch. I had a terrible haircut. A few months later, spring came. I got worse before I got better, but one day I started to heal. And though we graduated, and scattered ourselves all over the globe, my housemates were there for me through it all.

●

Perhaps you've heard about a movement that's unfolding in the United States and Europe. It's called the New Monasticism. Across the country and beyond, Christians are moving in together and exploring what it means to be parts of the body of Christ. It's a way of life that seems new, but draws on the ancient practices of monks in the early Church. Among the movement's tenets are a commitment to moving into disadvantaged neighborhoods, an emphasis on hospitality, and a commitment to sharing resources with those who have need.

The nine months I spent with my second family in that old house were my first introduction to the work of intentional community. It wasn't New Monasticism to the letter, but it certainly was an introduction to a new way of life, and one that was radically life changing. And while the title of this book is *It's Not All About You*, I have to admit that a lot of it *was* about me. It was about my learning to live with other people at a level of vulnerability that the rest of society reserves for only the most intimate or romantic relationships. It was about dealing with all the unexpected emotional gunk that came out of that intentionality. It was about opening my eyes and heart to other people's loneliness. That year I realized in full force that some people in our society are more readily upheld as having been made in the image of God than others. What a tragedy, for God and for the church.

@**Kristen** *Wow! Jonason mentions the "tragedy, for God and for the church" when we decide who is or isn't made in God's image. Tragedy indeed.*

I was very active in social justice work during college. I was even the co-chair of a big student group called the Social Justice Committee. So why, when asked to write about what fuels my desire to live a life of justice and service to others, did my mind come to rest on the memory of a snowy Sunday morning in Grand Rapids? A Sunday morning where all I was trying to do was get to church?

If there is one reason, I think it is more of an emotional than a rational one. There, in that household, were some people who came to know me. And what a beautiful and critical thing it is to know others and to be known by them. While I do believe, as many contemplative thinkers and writers do, that God can be most present with us when we are alone,[1] I believe also that we are created to live in deep and right relationships with other people.

@**Kristen** *One young adult finds that as she focuses on getting to know other people, she too experiences personal growth.*

Through our communities we find the strength to confront the sadness and brokenness of the world. Life in a city in the United States today has a lot of challenges. There is crime, racism, poverty, and ugliness. But there are also so many opportunities for reconciliation and restoration. God works through us, working together, to build his kingdom here on earth.

A little more than two years after the day that I didn't go to church, I moved into another 100-year-old house in another city in the Midwestern United States. This time, it wasn't a three-story mansion. This time, the house belonged to me. I signed a mortgage and received the key. I'm still working on making it a home. It helps to have three households of neighbors nearby, three groups of people with whom I pray and eat and worship. We are married and single, in our twenties and in our sixties, childbearing and childless. When we get together we talk a lot. Sometimes we forget to pray until the very end of our meeting. But I have a feeling that God is present among us the entire time. We are telling our stories, learning to be vulnerable, and starting to talk about how we can make a difference in our neighborhood. We even swear in front of each other once in a while.

Amy's conversation partner was Kristen Walling. She read Amy's essay and sent the tweets you see in the margins. Find Kristen's essay, "Stealing Back the Future," on page 107.

Looking Around

Resource Suggestions from the Author and Editors

The Irresistible Revolution—by Shane Claiborne

The Wisdom of Stability—by Jonathan Wilson-Hartgrove

New Monasticism—www.newmonasticism.org

Want to try out an intentional community for yourself? Check out internships and apprenticeships at www. rebaplacefellowship.org, or browse the possibilities at www. communityofcommunities.info and mvs.mennonite.net

Notes

[1]For a poignant illustration of this truth, check out Tanya Davis' performance of her poem "How to Be Alone," filmed and edited by Andrea Dorfman, available at http://www.youtube.com/watch?v=k7X7sZzSXYs.

Questions \ for Discussion and Contemplation

1 Can you think of a community you have been a part of that has made you more "you"? What made that community work?

2 If real community does indeed make us stronger, why do we as human beings often insist on doing so much "on our own"?

3 Why is it often so difficult, do you think, for people to truly see something divine in one another? To recognize our common humanity?

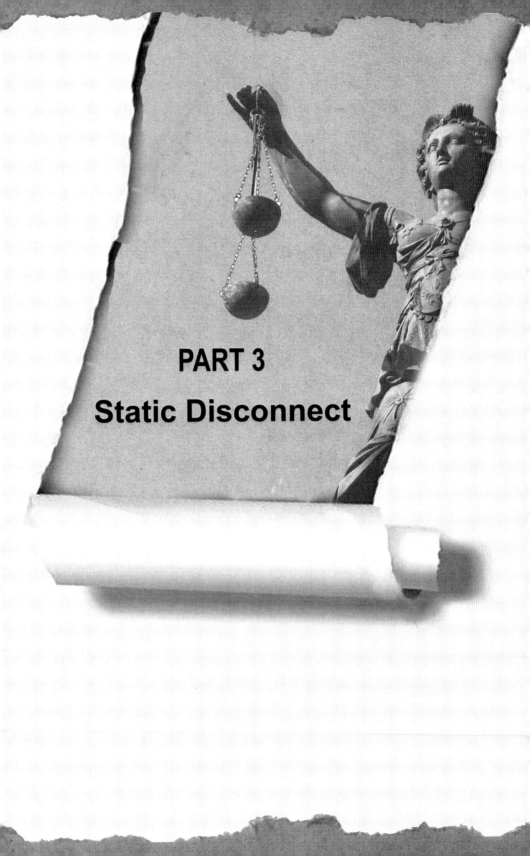

PART 3

Static Disconnect

10

Frontera

DAN MILLIS

Man, what an idiot. I could barely hear myself scream, "Souuuundgardeeeeeeeennn!" through my earplugs. Whatever was so great about that goon squad making licking gestures between their fingers and strutting around on stage, I've forgotten by now. I just remember it was a hot July night in Phoenix, Lollapalooza '96, my first concert. I had no idea where my friends were. I just knew I was smashed between a million other sweat-drenched people, they had quit hosing the crowd off a while ago, someone was smoking pot, it would be a while before Metallica came on, and I was going to pass out if I didn't get some water soon.

Besides snaking the occasional candy fish or gumball from the bulk foods aisle at Smith's grocery, I'd never really stolen anything before. But I'd never really been thirsty before either. Dizzy and weak, I felt the first twinges of panic as I stumbled my way through the tightly packed crowd toward the refreshment stands. *Shit*—they were closed already, all of them. There must have been somewhere in those fairgrounds to buy a Gatorade or get a drink of water, but panic pushed me to more immediate action.

From behind some people still mesmerized by power chords and bass lines, I snuck up, grabbed their water bottle, and chugged most of it. I dropped it, not caring if they noticed or not, and wandered further into the crowd. The next guy caught me in mid-gulp sucking on his gallon jug. "Oh, sorry, I thought it was mine," I muttered in response to his angry look, and again I stumbled away. Why the hell didn't I just ask someone? It's not that hard: "Dude, I'm dizzy, can I have a sip of your water please?" I've thought a lot about it since then, puzzled by my irrational, spineless desperation.

About ten years later I met a whole slew of thirsty people in desperate, irrational situations. They, however, were anything but spineless.

There was a man whose name I don't even know, and who I only spoke with for a few minutes, whose selfless heroism I'll never forget. This is what I wrote about it in one of the e-mails I sent to friends and family:[1]

> [T]he group of four young men, a woman, and her two toddlers were on the verge of disaster. Two of the men and the four-year-old boy were vomiting. If you're severely dehydrated, can't hold fluids down, and in the desert heat, you stand little chance. The four-year-old boy and his two-year-old sister were both deaf. Their parents wanted to bring them north, where they would have better opportunities to take care of them. Their father was wearing crappy dress shoes. They had come across a group of migrants helping a man with a twisted and swollen ankle. The father noticed the injured man was wearing shoes inadequate for the desert. He traded him his athletic shoes for the injured man's crappy dress shoes—the same shoes that maybe caused the injury! We're not talking about a cop or a boy scout; this is a dehydrated, desperate man with a young wife and two disabled toddlers with him, lost in the desert. And he still gave the shoes off his feet for a fellow person in need! We know this story is true, because we had seen that same group, and we recognized the shoes as being those of the injured man.

Thirst is a constant companion in the Sonora desert, whether you're on the Mexico or Arizona side, or somewhere in between. That crisp, 2,000-mile line on the maps you grew up with is a myth, and always has been. Since its establishment, the "border" between the U.S. and Mexico has been better described by its Spanish synonym—*frontera*. For 350 years, the red-skinned people of this frontier have hosted uninvited brown and white-skinned people, first Spanish then also English-speaking, looking for not much more than a living and a drink of water. All of this "secure our broken borders" crap is a decidedly new phenomenon, one that has wreaked havoc on fragile lands and livelihoods in the last decade or two. Since then, the walls, the armed *federales* of the Border Patrol, and the morons whose wives named them "Minutemen" have forced people looking for work and water deeper into the dry, dry desert.

Many never emerge from its thirsty grip. According to a recent ACLU study, 5,600 have died since 1994. Instead of letting laborers pass safely through our ports-of-entry, Ellis Island style, the U.S. government response has been to try to wall them out. While celebrating the twentieth anniversary of the fall of the Berlin Wall, the feds continue building a much longer and deadlier wall here at home. Six hundred fifty counterproductive miles have been built so far. Walls and Border Patrol (known here as *la Migra*) have made the trek longer and more complicated, and most pay a smuggler thousands to guide them, with prices skyrocketing. Workers can't cross back and forth anymore for visits, so instead they're sending for their families to come join them in the U.S. More women and children are running the gauntlet of sand, sun, and snakes, and those fortunate enough to make it often find themselves walled in, unable to afford the emotional or monetary price of another crossing. That's right—we're walling people *in*, not out. I'm

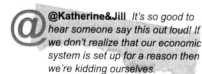

no conspiracy theorist, but at the time of this writing, the feds' diabolical goal is to have 666 miles of border barriers completed in the next several months. I shit you not, 666 Satanic miles.

So, besides the prospect of some sort of Beelzebubbalicious border plot, I guess the real question at issue here is, "Who cares?" Why should you or I bother to entangle ourselves in an ever-evolving clusterfuck, with drug cartel shootouts on one side, armed neo-nazis amassing on the other, leaving those in the middle with few options but duck-and-cover? Number of the Beast border wall aside, the answer, for me at least, is spiritual.

I'm not talking about Jesus. And though *La Virgen de Guadalupe* is everywhere around here—from trailside shrines where migrants leave her offerings days into their journey, to wife-beater tank top silk screens, even my truck's air freshener— I'm not talking about his mom, either. The closest church to my old house just south of Tucson is *La Misión San Xavier del Bac,* which was founded not just before Arizona was part of the U.S., but before the U.S. ever existed; (seventy-six years before, to be exact.) The spirits at work in the borderlands have a way of predating notions we can grasp, notions such as Jesus and his church.

●

Matt was a good friend and fellow volunteer with a slow Jersey drawl and a darker, skinnier version of the Luke Perry look about him. His wasn't your "standard faith-based hippy approach to border humanitarian aid," and his unique ideas got him in trouble with the old-schoolers. I remember when he called me up one February night and was like,"Yo, so you know that girl they been lookin' for? At the Sams meeting they said she got left at some platforms."

"Oh, great, he wants to do a search," I thought. I made some excuse not to go, since searches always end up being more trouble than they're worth. We only get fragmentary information—they crossed at Sásabe; we left him near the mountain, next to the power line. Then a gaggle of retirees and recent college grads heads out to some random spot with a mountain and a power line in this "bajillion"-acre wilderness and does well if they don't create more victims. I remember one of my favorite older Samaritan ladies falling off a log and bruising her rib in the remote stretches of Sycamore Canyon, and almost losing a couple guys from the Guatemalan consulate out on the open range of the Tohono O'odham nation.

"You know that place down off Arivaca Road at milepost 7, those concrete slabs back there? I'm gonna head out there tomorrow."

Nah, I couldn't make it. But the platform search wasn't Matt's only crazy idea that day.

"I'm almost done fillin' up the Gatorades for that storage box I got—you know, the big plastic ones? And I got food packs and socks and first aid stuff for it. So can I give it to you sometime to put out?"

He had been talking about his food box idea for a while, and I didn't like it. I figured a bunch of food would just sit around in the desert and rot, or animals would get it and spread it everywhere, or the box would fill up with rain water, or someone would gank it. Plus, lugging a big-ass box down cactus-strewn trails didn't sound like fun to me. But Matt had been visionary in his water drops. He discovered some of the most effective locations and techniques for putting clean gallon jugs of drinking water out on migrant trails, so the folks we never found could still at least find water. We kept track of each jug, labeling them with dates, GPS waypoint locations, and a *"Buena suerte!"* Every week or so we'd come around again to each spot and check up on them, picking up waste and replacing water found by night-walking migrants. I agreed to give his box idea a chance, and he went out on a futile search for a dead little girl.

Meanwhile, I'd been hanging out with Max a lot. A hilarious, hard-drinking, bona fide man in black (Johnny, not Tommy), Max was one of the few Mexican-Americans heavily involved in the local border humanitarian aid movement. I had told him about Matt's supply box idea, and asked if he wanted to help me put it out on a border trail.

"Cool, man," he said, in typical *suave* Max fashion.

I knew a spot where two busy migrant trails converged, which would be our best bet for getting food to hungry travelers before javelinas, coyotes, or mold could get to it. But, like I said, hauling that heavy mother down a mile of steep gnarly trail wasn't going to work. So I found a dirt road on the map that dead-ended pretty close to the fork in the trail, at the mouth of a canyon. On the map, it looked like we could walk a shortcut up this canyon, but we'd never been before. Two or three weeks after Matt's call and fruitless search, Max, two brand-new volunteers and I were bushwhacking up a canyon with his heavy plastic bin, rosary beads taped to it and *Buena suertes* and other stuff scrawled in marker all over it. For the new volunteers, it was their very first patrol.

My blog post the next day, "Border Eclipse," went like this:

Right now I am trying to decide if I want to write this. I think I do, because you need to know. And you need to do something. We all do.

Yesterday afternoon three young volunteers and I were on a No More Deaths patrol in a remote desert canyon. We were dropping off water, food, blankets, shoes and socks along some remote migrant trails. Walking up the canyon, I saw some green shoes, and, thinking they looked pretty new, began to yell, as we always do, "Hola, hola! Tenemos agua, comida, somos de la iglesia, blah blah..." I only got to the second "hola" before I saw her teeth, and spun around, and told my friends, "Stop."

I had never found someone dead in the desert before. The feeling is horrendous; so ugly, frustrating, tragic. I just looked at my feet and said "Goddammit." I'm still mad.

Josseline was only fourteen years old. She was from El Salvador, heading to the West Coast to reunite with family members there. I can't stop thinking of all the freshmen I taught at VVS—she could have been one of them.

VVS is an international boarding school where I taught Spanish and outdoor sports to high schoolers. Josseline had been missing for three weeks; God knows how long she'd been lying there. She was the girl Matt had been looking for. He hadn't found her; he never came close. But his idea, his spirit, led us straight to her.

●

If finding someone dead is tough, getting the lifeless body out of the wilderness is a nightmare. Long story short, it involves lengthy waits in less-than-comfortable circumstances, bumbling, insensitive cops, gruesome sights, smells, and feelings—both emotional and tactile. The only things you might call "positive" about the whole experience were that we had time to get the supply box out to the trail, and we knew who she was before the cops ever arrived. By the time we finally got her back to the dirt road, the sun had set. A full lunar eclipse was on the rise, and would accompany us all the way home.

A certain darkness remained long after the eclipse receded. Understandably shaken, Max and I headed out to the migrant trails again two days later, hoping the water we had left there would quench our own therapeutic needs along with the thirst of those who walk the desert. Instead, federal law enforcement officials issued me a littering ticket that day. Yes, littering. We said leaving water for those dying of thirst is *not* littering, and showed them the five milk crates full of trash we'd picked up along the way. Unimpressed, the officers said we weren't allowed to leave anything without a permit, and we weren't allowed to pick anything up without a permit either. Max even showed them the missing persons flier with Josseline's photos, speaking truth to power, only to be shouted down, "Good! I'm glad you found her! Now go step next to the vehicle!"

I was the first of eighteen volunteers to be ticketed for littering. Two of us have been convicted in federal court, while charges against the other sixteen were dropped. Both of us "convicted litterers" are in the drawn-out process of appealing. But I learned my lesson. Any faith I ever had in the criminal justice system has evaporated—like a jug of fresh water spilled on the hot desert floor.

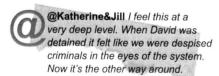

@Katherine&Jill *I feel this at a very deep level. When David was detained it felt like we were despised criminals in the eyes of the system. Now it's the other way around.*

Despite federal attempts to stop us, the desert work continues. Besides inadvertently leading us to Josseline, Matt's supply boxes eventually revolutionized the way No More Deaths provides aid supplies along the border. We often fill a box up with food, and it is totally empty the next day. Dozens of supply boxes have been deployed in a variety of remote locations, providing a little nourishment where before none was to be had. Matt eventually quit border activism, burned by strife within the movement, or maybe just burnt out. I would see him in town walking his pit bull or driving his shuttle bus, and wonder if he knows the depth of his contribution.

Max also moved on, first to NYC and then the Bay, still working toward a better world. The last time I saw him he had quit drinking and was doing one of those stupid hippy cleanse diets, but he was giggly as ever. We didn't discuss the dirty details of those two particular days in the desert, the curse of the dead, the spite of the feds. Instead we talked about Babo.

Baboquivari Mountain is a gigantic stone monolith that reaches nearly 8,000 feet in elevation, the top 1,000+ of which are walls of sheer rock. Less than twenty miles from México, Babo marks the crossroads of the Mexican, O'odham, and U.S. nations, and can be seen from virtually anywhere No More Deaths operates. Sacred to the O'odham people, it is so tall and steep that it wags its stony finger at you when you drag its Google Earth map back and forth. When I first started volunteering, I figured it must have been named for an Irishman—Bob O'Keevry. I had the pronunciation right, but learned the proper spelling from the Mexican bottled water— brought to the U.S. by migrants—that sports Babo's name and likeness across its label.

When a friend and I went to climb Babo for my first time, I was already a little nervous about it. My nervousness turned to dread about three-quarters of the way up the trail, but not for my own well-being. Somewhere near or above 6,000 feet elevation, we came to a cross trail, one we had not anticipated. "What the hell is this other trail doing...," I had begun to ponder, when it hit me: "Oh shit, this is a *migrant* trail." The thought of migrants, among them women and young girls like Josseline, trying to negotiate this steep, unforgiving terrain at night made my stomach sink. But as the feds make it tougher and tougher to cross, people are heading to rougher and rougher country to avoid them.

Frontera

My apprehension mostly dissolved when we hit the summit of Baboquivari Peak. I was finally standing on top of that omnipresent point, after spending five years in its shadow. The sacredness of this site is not only seen in the boundless, tri-national view, or the native prayer sticks left there by tribal worshipers. It is felt. People also leave important keepsakes in a sealed green steel ammo can, along with photos of those who have passed on. Among them, someone had left a photo of Josseline. She was already there by the time I summited that sacred stone—maybe she'd been there all along.

I guess it's possible that my involvement in this border water bonanza could be a subliminal reaction to some subconscious guilt trip about my water steal-a-palooza years ago, but I doubt it. Now if I get thirsty, I don't hesitate to ask for a drink of water, and no one has hesitated yet in providing it.

●

● Dan's conversation partners were Katherine Bell and Jill Delaney. They read Dan's essay and sent the tweets you see in the margins. Find Katherine and Jill's essay, "The Slow Examples of Lifetimes" on page 115.

●

Editorial Note: *In the time since Dan wrote his essay, he's written to say: "I won my case! The 9th Circuit Court of Appeals ruled 2-1 in favor of our argument that life-saving water does not constitute 'litter.' The prosecution has thrown in the towel, meaning that they will not pursue this to the level of the U.S. Supreme Court, and have recommended that my friend Walt's 'littering' conviction also be overturned!" Available at: http://www.nytimes.com/2010/09/27/us/27water.html*

Looking Around
Resource Suggestions from the Author and Editors

Humanitarian Crisis: Migrant Deaths at the U.S.–Mexico Border
by Maria Jimenez, American Civil Liberties Union, October 2009
http://www.aclu.org/files/pdfs/immigrants/
humanitariancrisisreport.pdf

The Death of Josseline: Immigration Stories from the Arizona-Mexico Borderlands by Margaret Regan, Beacon Press, 2010

To volunteer, or for more info, see the NMD Web site:
www.nomoredeaths.org
or look up "No More Deaths" on Facebook

Notes

[1] I've since posted these e-mails to a blog—www.borderstoked.com

Questions \ for Discussion and Contemplation

1 Do you know what it is to be truly thirsty? To need water so much that you'd do *anything* for it? Has your belly ever gone so long without being filled that you'd eat *anything*? Have you ever known such desperation?

2 Do stories like Josseline's matter? Does such deep pain make a difference in your life?

3 What is it about Dan's stories that reminds you, or perhaps challenges you to discover, that it is *NOT* all about you?

11

Coffee Can Change

JENNIFER FISCHER

Can an empty coffee can change the world? When I was a little girl, I thought so.

My parents tell me they came home one day in my early years to find coffee grounds all over the kitchen floor. I'd been watching TV, and there was a commercial about feeding starving children. My response was to empty the coffee can and take it door to door to collect money to help. I believed that act would make a difference in the life of another child.

I'm much older now and have a greater understanding of the world. I've traveled to many other countries, even living in Egypt for six months. I've worked for various non-profits and now have two companies of my own. Do I still believe that an empty coffee can change the world? Yes. And here's why...

Growing up in Texas, I had a huge poster of a grand piano on the stage at Carnegie Hall and dreamed of one day playing there. In the process of pursuing that dream, I discovered that the thing you think you want the most in the world sometimes does not make you happy at all.

I loved playing the piano and worked very hard to get a piano scholarship, not only because being a pianist was, I thought, my "calling," but also because it would get me out of the small Texas town I'd been raised in. When I landed this scholarship to a very good school in Indiana, I went, convinced it would be perfect.

It was not. To my surprise, I did not like being in an intense environment in which music became war. I began to *hate* playing the piano. The joy I found in music was disappearing. Piano was no longer a form of expression and meditation. The price, for me, was too high. My dream of playing at Carnegie Hall and teaching piano at the collegiate level was not worth the loss of love and joy in playing.

Also, the school was quite conservative, and I was unhappy. During Christmas break of my second year, I told my parents I was dropping out. My parents, wise and wonderful, were supportive, but also told me I couldn't live at home because I made the decision to leave school and a scholarship behind. My parents helped me get set up an apartment in San Antonio, and I worked as a nanny and waitress and delved into school research. This time, I would make a better choice.

I ended up at Sarah Lawrence College—a small, very liberal school outside of New York City. It was expensive, but fit me perfectly: fifteen students per class and a curriculum that focused on personalized student research and papers. I loved it!

At Sarah Lawrence, I focused on sociology and international relations. I took my first course about the Middle East—and was completely captivated. Wanting to encourage my obvious interest, my professor suggested that I go to Egypt and study there. I jumped in with both feet, going to Cairo six weeks before the study abroad program started. Soon, I found myself in a strange country, knowing no one and not one word of the local language, in an empty apartment with no hot water and no food, and I cried: *"What the hell was I thinking?"* Somehow, though, I got through that first night and even traveled to other parts of the Middle East: Lebanon: Jordan, Syria, Jerusalem, the West Bank. The experience was amazing and difficult, overwhelming and wonderful.

The experience would complete change my life—I would meet Ramon, the man I would decide to share my life with, raise a family with, and run two businesses with. Aside from meeting Ramon, the most significant experience of the entire six months was the few days I spent in Jerusalem and the West Bank. It gave me a new purpose for my life. I became convinced that I needed to work for peace between Israelis and Palestinians.

First, I had to finish school and get a job. I benefited so much from my time at Sarah Lawrence, yet attending a very unique and small school that does not have tests or traditional grades or majors has its own challenges in the work place. After graduation I moved to Boston with Ramon and started looking for work. In the end, it came down to a choice between two very different jobs: an Americorps job doing conflict resolution work with youth, and a secretarial position at a construction company. You might guess that I took the Americorps job, but I didn't.

I had a lot of student loans from Sarah Lawrence, and Boston is expensive. The Americorps job paid so little that they often had to help students find subsidized housing and apply for food stamps. The construction company paid quite well for a first-time job out of college. The weight of the student loans felt overwhelming, so I took the secretarial job. At the time, it seemed like the best decision for me, and I did meet a very good friend at that job, and the work was easy, but was not fulfilling or engaging. In the end I learned that sometimes you have to do something in order to learn that you don't need to do it.

While there, I began applying to graduate schools. I applied to Brown University and M.I.T. and wanted to apply to Harvard, but I convinced myself that I wouldn't get in, so I didn't want to try.

What a stupid way to live! This is the very mentality that I "unteach" my students now. Luckily, I had someone in my life that told me how stupid I was being. Specifically, I recall Ramon saying something like, "For someone who is smart, you can be really dumb. Of course you'll get into Harvard and if you want, I'll pay the $70 application fee if that's the problem." He called my bluff.

@**Marc** *I like Ramon's role in this story. Supportive and encouraging—sounds like the kind of partner we all might learn from.*

Of course, it wasn't the money. It was the fear of rejection. I had dropped out of college at one point. I worked as a secretary. I never did prestigious internships because I spent summers and winter breaks as a waitress to earn money for college, books, and living expenses. How could I possibly get in? Well, that is the challenge of admission essays, isn't it? You have to write about why you should get in. I sent my transcripts, and I wrote a passionate essay about my experiences in the Middle East and how they altered my life.

Much to my surprise, and to Ramon's non-surprise, I got in. My mom cried. I cried. Out of joy, of course—then the reality of the expense set in. I would have to, once again, take out a huge student loan to pay for it, but do you say no to Harvard because you don't have the money? I think not.

On September 12, 2001 (with the whole world having been rocked by the events of the day before), my campus job began. I was the Outreach Assistant for the Outreach Center of the Center for Middle Eastern Studies. The Outreach Center provided "resources and support for educators and the general public on topics related to the Middle East and Islam/Muslim communities through a free lending library, on-line resources, curriculum kits and public events and workshops."

After the devastating events of 9/11, everyone wanted to learn about Islam and Arab culture. People had a lot of misinformation and a lot of misguided hatred and anger. In the Middle East, I had met a lot of wonderful, generous people and experienced a very positive, loving, and open practice of Islam. (Of course, I also met some people who were not nice, who judged me harshly for being American, and who practiced a very rigid form of Islam; however I also meet similar individuals regularly in the United States, and see Christianity practiced in a variety of ways and used for a variety of purposes.)

Through my work at the Outreach Center, I realized that sharing my firsthand knowledge about the region was a form of peacemaking—an *important* form of peacemaking. I could build bridges between Muslims and non-Muslims. I could help people separate the individuals that perpetrated the awful acts of 9/11 from the millions of Muslims throughout the world who found that act to be very contrary to their religious beliefs. I realized that being a peacemaker did not necessarily involve official diplomacy or treaties, but could be as simple as breaking down stereotypes. This work experience combined with academic research and my personal spiritual practices shifted my conceptions of peacemaking. Previously, I entered the program thinking I would end up living in the Middle East doing work "on the ground" that promoted peace between Israelis and Palestinians, and working for a just solution to the conflict.

I discovered that role didn't make sense for me, but not because of fear (as some may think), for I did spend part of the summer in 2002 in the Middle East working to improve my Arabic and learn more about the region. Rather, for me as a white, middle-class American who had lived a life of substantial privilege and comfort (in regards to much of the world and particularly in regards to a war-torn area), it no longer felt right to go and tell other people, who had suffered things I could never imagine, that they should get along for the "greater good," so to speak.

I discovered my very deep-felt need to be a peacemaker was more appropriately met through my work at the Outreach Center and through working with organizations focused on promoting a just American foreign policy toward the conflict and the region in general.

I was also beginning to learn that opportunities for peacemaking are all around us. A couple of years earlier, a friend had taken me to hear Thich Nhat Hanh, a Vietnamese monk, speak, and gave me *Being Peace*, one of his many books. Thay (as he is often called) writes, "If we are peaceful, if we are happy, we can blossom like a flower, and everyone in our family, our entire society, will benefit from our peace."

This is now my life philosophy. I understand that being loving and caring to those around me, even if I am frustrated, tired, or angry, can be an act of peacemaking and that being happy and fulfilled is critical if you want to make a positive difference in the world.

I may earn much less money, struggle with issues of health insurance, and make financial (and personal) sacrifices at times, but I love my work. I love the tiny little house that amazing circumstances allowed Ramon and me to purchase. I love the community that I am building. A friend watches my son Sky for free and her daughters attend our summer camp for free. I've swapped piano lessons for laundry. I have been overwhelmed by the generosity of others, such as a wonderful family giving me their piano. I try to show the same generosity to others, as much as I can, whenever I can. I've given time and money, when I felt that I had neither, and somehow I can always pay the bills. Karma?

My daily involvement in working to positively impact my community gives meaning to my life and is a constant reminder that "it isn't all about me." My students sustain me and, when I am particularly exhausted or broke or overwhelmed, I think of them.

@Marc *My favorite aspect of this piece? Jenni had these ideas as a kid, and, despite a circuitous route, actually followed through. Inspiring* :)

I think of Gabriel. He drove me crazy. He always needed attention and was a major distraction. He pushed back at me every chance he had. Then, we started an animation project using WWE action figures (he loved wrestling) and I saw a light go on. He became less and less of a distraction and more of an asset. By the time we were editing the film, which can be a tedious process for adults, much less Elementary School students, Gabriel wouldn't leave my side and begged to keep editing and working on the film, even while the rest of the class was outside playing. And then one day, he said, "Miss Jen, when I grow up, if I have a daughter, I want to name her Jennifer." Imagine that.

At that moment, I knew unequivocally that I was doing something with my life that had value and that all the sacrifices were absolutely worth it

Johnny was more of an athlete than an artist, but through theater and performance pieces, he showed a completely different side of himself. Always a joy to teach, I was surprised when his father told me that prior to attending our program, Johnny got in trouble a lot. Now, his father tells me, Johnny wants to be a teacher, is focused at school, and helps his coach.

Giving back to the world and nurturing students such as Johnny and Gabriel, who will hold their own personal "coffee cans," feels pretty damn good.

At the after-school program I run, we have a club called "Be the Change" (inspired by Gandhi). The students literally decorate an empty coffee can and ask their fellow students and parents to give what they can.

That empty coffee can makes a difference. Miguel's actions show how much of a difference. Last year, one of the "Be the Change" projects involved a toy drive, in addition to the coffee can change. The toys were for children living in domestic violence shelters. Miguel himself had previously been in foster care, was one of many children living in a tiny space at home, and new toys were not something he often (or ever) had. Yet, Miguel brought toys for the toy drive. He brought several stuffed animals—worn and dirty, but so valuable to him. His sincere act of generosity overwhelmed me.

Those are the stories I go back to when my coffee can feels, somehow, simultaneously empty and heavy, and I want to put it down. I think of Johnny and Gabriel and Miguel and I realize that I am still (and will always be) that little girl with a coffee can doing what I can in my small corner of the world to make a positive difference. What's great now is that others have seen me hold my can and are holding cans of their own.

@**Marc** *The "coffee can" image is great, esp. because I'm a daily coffee drinker. Now, every morning, my cup will remind me of Jenni's story.* :)

●

● Jennifer's conversation partner was Marc Istook. He read Jenni's essay and sent the tweets you see in the margins. Find Marc's essay, "Call," on page 3.

Looking Around
Resource Suggestions from the Author and Editors

Santa Clarita Valley Film Festival—http://scvfilmfestival.com/

Questions \for Discussion and Contemplation

1 Do you believe you can make a difference? If you do, how? Or, if you do not, why not?

2 What can you do to "positively impact" the world around you?

3 Do you have a "coffee can"? What is it?

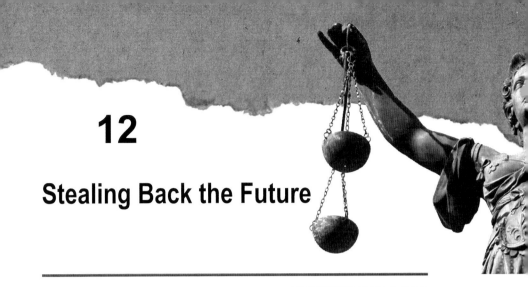

12

Stealing Back the Future

KRISTEN WALLING

It is said that walking through "The Door of No Return" sealed their fate; in reality, their fates were decided long before. At any given time, anywhere from 600 to 1,000 people would typically be confined to the dungeons, usually not much larger than fifteen feet by fifteen feet. At night, they slept on the cold, damp, rock floor. If they were extremely lucky, they may have been given a mat to sleep on; usually their only option was to pile on top of one another. They urinated into a thin track in the floor, no more than two inches wide, which carried the urine out to the ocean. There were boxes in the corners to defecate in, but they filled up quickly and were rarely emptied. To this day, visitors can see discoloration on the lower portion of the walls, indicating that the overflow excrement often piled two feet high. The only light that entered a dungeon came through a single peephole, too high on the wall for anyone to look out and see the water. Families were divided—men in one dungeon, women in another—and confined to these quarters for as little as two weeks or as long as six months. They were finally reunited with sunlight and each other upon walking through that immense and foreboding door, that gateway to the ships, which would carry them across the Atlantic to the Americas. On the next level up were the Governor's quarters, the rooms where he lived, conducted business, and raped his countless female victims. And above everything—above the pain, the suffering, the abuse, the despair, the disease, the seemingly endless torture—was the most haunting image of all.

Above it all, there sat a church.

It was during my semester abroad in Ghana that my program took me to visit Cape Coast Castle. During the tour, my guide discussed the history of the slave trade and explained how many of the slaves taken to the Americas were captured in Ghana and shuttled through this or another slave castle along the West African coast. Out of everything I heard and saw on the tour, I was most disturbed by the fact that the church sat directly above the male dungeons. It seemed unfathomable to me that people could worship and praise God in a place that was responsible for the atrocities suffered by hundreds of thousands of African men, women, and children. Not only did Christians allow slavery, but many supported it, benefited from it, and actively worked for it to remain as the reigning order. I could not figure out how such a thing had ever happened.

Walking around, I couldn't push several nagging questions out of my head: *If I had been here 400 years ago, what would I have done? Would I have recognized how terrible it was? If I did recognize it, would I have even cared? Would I have tried to do anything to stop it?* I wondered what things we consider status quo today that history will look back upon with disgust—the things we participate in, support, accept, or even just passively allow. I thought about how even with as much progress as we seem to think we've made in America, we still have to deal with racism, sexism, classism, homelessness, poverty, hunger, violence, sexual assault, strict immigration laws, lack of gay rights, and dozens of other injustices. I realized with disappointment that in 400 years, these will probably be the things everyone is appalled that we never stood up to protest. In reflecting on all of these questions and thoughts, I recalled a particular conversation from a job I had one summer.

@**Amy** *I once heard an activist say, "If you aren't fighting for civil rights now, you wouldn't have a generation ago, either." Yikes...*

I had been interning at a church, working primarily with the youth group. I met periodically for coffee throughout the summer with a particular staff member—I'll call him Jerry—who wanted to check in and find out how things were going, talk through the joys and frustrations of the job, and make sure that I was developing both spiritually and professionally. At the end of the summer we had a final meeting, one which I was anticipating to be similar to our other casual but intentional conversations. Jerry threw me a bit off guard when he asked me point blank what I felt was my call. It seemed like an easy enough question at first, so I answered right away. I began to ramble, "Well, I've thought about going to seminary, but lately I've been considering law school." He politely interrupted me but firmly said, "I didn't ask what you want to do. I asked what you believe your calling is."

I paused, thinking for a few moments longer about my answer. I started to speak again, but after stumbling around a few points I still wasn't making much sense. Jerry didn't say much, but I could tell he was waiting for me to elaborate. When I tried to get around the answer or shirk the question a bit, he kept prodding me for a more thought-out explanation. When I looked confusedly at him, he persisted that I answer the question. Amid growing frustration at myself for being unable to articulate my thoughts and with him for continuing to goad me for a more intentional answer, I worked myself to the brink of tears. I knew what he was asking, but I realized in that moment that I had no idea how I personally wanted to answer the question. Prior to that day, I don't think I had ever really been asked, and had therefore never been forced to reflect on what I truly felt called to do with my life. This realization launched my thoughts into chaos, where I suddenly felt like everything I had been doing that summer and everything I thought I was working toward in college was meaningless. If there was no intentional thought behind my actions, *what could* be the meaning of them? I had only ever thought through my life plan in terms of a career or a particular job, but never as part of fulfillment of a particular mission or purpose. It was obviously time to begin considering a different approach.

Recognizing my fragile (and, admittedly, rather hysterical) state, Jerry let me collect myself and then moved on with the conversation. But even years later, I continued to be frustrated by those few moments. His calm but stern approach had forced me to realize that I had some things to think about. I kept recounting the conversation in my head and trying to come up with the millions of other things I wished I had said. I remained dissatisfied with the answers I had been unable to give him at the time, and though I had finally started searching for an answer, I still never felt like I was getting anywhere close to discovering how I wanted to channel my passions into something with a purpose. And though remembering that conversation had driven me crazy for so long, I have ultimately grown grateful for the intentionality Jerry had in prodding me.

Eventually, I discovered that what actually made that conversation so powerful and resonant with me were not the specific questions that Jerry asked. Rather, what made that talk over coffee significant were the answers he demanded of me. He refused to let me get away with easy answers, so I also had to stop letting myself get away with them. While this had originally frustrated me, it was my annoyance and unrest that forced me to reconsider my values and change my course of action.

In much the same way, it is this idea of dissatisfaction that keeps me committed to my faith, to justice, to service, and to making all of these things intersect. I have so many friends who tell me they're turned off by organized religion because it is often bureaucratic, unwelcoming, biased, judgmental, or many other things. And, you know, in many ways I really can't blame them. While I personally grew up in a family of several generations of church-goers and remain strongly committed to my faith, I have to be honest: I'm not sure I would be all that interested in today's church if it had not been for this upbringing.

It seems ironic, this idea that the church is so far from perfect that I want to remain active in, involved with, and connected to it. But then I ask myself: Where would we be if everybody who cared just got up and left? What if nobody ever stayed around to ask the tough questions (or, rather, demand better answers)? What keeps me going is the knowledge that if nobody dares ask the questions, nobody else is ever going to have to look for the answers. To the people in our generation who feel that the church has become irrelevant or unresponsive to the needs of today's young adults, I challenge that notion. Maybe it's true that right now the right questions aren't being asked, but it's got to start somewhere. I can't imagine a better group of people to get things started than those who are frustrated with the way things are and are ready to start redefining the way we as a society approach things.

@Amy *Maybe the best thing education can do for us is to make us aware of our assumptions and show us how to change them.*

In today's world, it's really easy to get distracted by everything going on and forget what we were ever trying to do in the first place. New technology, which allows us to do more things more quickly, also means that we're *expected* to do more things more quickly. And, furthermore, we can't even just *do* things for their own purpose anymore. We have to make sure we don't forget to tweet it or text it or add it to our newsfeed so that everybody we know (and their moms and cousins and friends and coworkers and neighbors and classmates) can find out about it and share it with everyone they know. We document everything in this manner, operating under the assumption that it's really important. Yet if someone were to ask us why we had chosen to do a particular thing, we might find that we do not actually have an answer to give. It is the moments like these that are dangerous. It is in these moments when we lack purpose and intentionality that we allow the slave castles to be built, the genocide to occur, the discriminatory law to pass unchallenged, the man on the street to go hungry. But it doesn't have to be this way.

I have lately drawn some inspiration from the television show *Leverage* on TNT, which features a Robin Hood–esque band of thieves and con artists turned good guys. Each of their cons usually involves stealing something back from or pulling a trick on the real villains in order to get people to do the right thing (in their words, they "provide leverage"). In most episodes, leader and mastermind Nathan Ford concocts a scam that seems utterly impossible to his team members, and then he tells them, "Let's go steal us a [*fill-in-the-blank*]." The thing he wants them to steal is always something completely outlandish: a baseball stadium, a concert, a mountain. In one of my favorite episodes involving a manipulative television psychic, Nate's standard line becomes, "Let's go steal us the future." That line has resonated with me because I feel like it articulates perfectly where our generation is right now.

We can see a glimpse of where things are headed, but we do not like what we see. We're frustrated and tired of the present, and we feel like the future does not even belong to us anymore. We are yearning for something better, something meaningful. But if we're upset, we need to be the ones to take things back into our own possession; we can't sit around and wait for everyone else. We need to hold accountable those around us—our politicians, our clergy, our colleagues, our classmates, our neighbors, and our friends—and remind them that every thing they do should be done with purpose and intentionality. No institution such as a government, a church body, or a community organization can thrive for very long without a clear vision and objective. We have to think of our generation in the same way. We must find the things we want to be a part of, even if we may be frustrated with their current state, and find ways to challenge the *status quo*. We have to be willing to ask difficult questions, and we must refuse to accept answers that just don't seem to be cutting it. We must remember to ask ourselves why we do the things we do, what we're hoping to accomplish, and if we're really going about it the best way. If we can do these things, we just may be able to steal back the future.

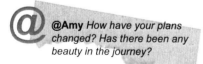

@**Amy** *How have your plans changed? Has there been any beauty in the journey?*

● Kristen's conversation partner was Amy Jonason. She read Kristen's essay and sent the tweets you see in the margins. Find Amy's essay, "The Day We Didn't Go to Church," on page 78.

Looking Around
Resource Suggestions from the Author and Editors

Peace Corps—www.peacecorps.gov

Kristen's blog—http://KristenInMadagascar.blogspot.com

Questions \ for Discussion and Contemplation

1 As Kristen writes, "If I had been there 400 years ago, what would I have done?...Would I have tried to do anything to stop it?" What would you have done?

2 What frustrates you the most about the world today? Not about your own life, but the world? Are you prepared to do something about it?

3 What future for the church and for the world do *you* want to "steal back"?

13

The Slow Examples of Lifetimes

KATHERINE BELL AND JILL DELANEY

Editorial Note: Katherine and Jill live and work on the Yakama Indian Reservation in White Swan, Wash. They have learned there that stories are everything—that stories are how Native Americans remember, instruct, live, and have hope. It is out of this rich tradition of indigenous storytelling—and in that style—that they share their thoughts on what it means to remember that the world and its people are not our own.

"How can you do it? Why do it? If those questions are answerable for either a monk or a Plains resident [or two women from Yakama Christian Mission], they can't be answered in a few quick words but in the slow example of a lifetime. The questioner must take the process of endless waiting into account, as well as the pull of the sea change, of conversion."

Kathleen Norris, Dakota

Remember

It is said that in the beginning God imagined and brought each vivid image into being and named it all beloved goodness: land and water, trees and mountains, critters and folks.

It is remembered that in the early days, those whose bodies were broken with toil would be made whole again through an act of exodus and given a land of sweetness and substance.

It was recorded that during the years that followed, they walked through veil and shadow, led by an outstretched hand. The land they descended upon, however, had already chosen its people. It didn't seem to matter. Another exodus began.

It was documented that in 1855 the people were gathered to sign an agreement between nations: between themselves and those who were descending into their land. There was no creation that took place, merely destruction. Word spread. A place reserved for their kind. Leave taking, departure, a tearing apart of their very selves.

It was proclaimed that in 1863 all slaves in Rebel territory were emancipated; they were set free. Two years later the 13th Amendment to the Constitution of the United States of America outlawed slavery.

It was voted upon and approved in 1870 that the United States would no longer create nations within the Nation; the folks who came here would no longer make treaties with the folks who were already here. *Note: Native Americans were not allowed to vote until nearly fifty years later.*

It was recorded on the cornerstone laid on Bedloe's Island: "Give me your tired, your poor, your huddled masses yearning to breathe free, the wretched refuse of your teeming shore, send these, the homeless, tempest-tost to me..." Whom did they have in mind?

It was termed "La Primera Intervención Estadounidense en México" (The First American intervention in Mexico), the Mexican-American War. Residents of the Southwest had new owners.

It was well known that in 1920 the full rights of citizenship were bestowed upon another group of folks.

It was sung before it ever took place: "We have come over a way that with tears has been watered, / We have come, treading our path through the blood of the slaughtered, / Out from the gloomy past, / Till now we stand at last, / Where the white gleam of our bright star is cast."[1]

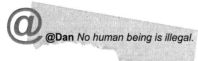
@Dan *No human being is illegal.*

It was broadcast through every possible medium that if you were (1) brown, (2) carpooled, (3) wore heavy hooded clothing, and (4) looked illegal you should carry your documents with you at all times in Arizona.

It is said that in the beginning God rejoiced and each vivid image was called into being and named beloved goodness.

Re-act

First come, first serve to settle on the new territory. They told the not-white-enough inhabitants that they had two years to pack their belongings and walk to their corral of land, herded like cattle. The news came swiftly like a passing breeze that licked their cheeks with an icy tongue, warning that those who refused would be slain. Two weeks were taken with the wind, and wagons on the horizon came with haste, abusing the agreement, homes, and land of the people. They were removed with the dust of the earth. Many years passed and they stuffed the newspapers full of pictures of half-starved babies with bulging, empty bellies. They portrayed a community who did not know how to take care of itself. Money lay idle, children went uneducated, and homes were unspeakably unlivable.

They smothered, restrained, and stained them with unwanted help. They took the children at six years old, saying it was for their own good. They were ripped from their parents' arms and ripped from their community. They were ripped from tradition, ripped from culture and stories, and ripped from existence. They cut their hair, changed their names, and taught them a new language, forcing them to forget everything of their wild life. Soon things grew all too familiar and those who grew up in the systems began sending their own children to the schools which had once taken them away. They did what they knew. Of generations and generations of children being taken and sent, they remembered.

They escaped from a land where their children were dying. The college professors, doctors, and scientists came to a place where labor in the three months of summer allowed them more income than their careers at home. They brought their families to a new home that would keep them alive and together. They that had high prestige became the lowest of low, dirt, filth like the clay that stained their clothes from the long journey. They heard of the endless possibilities and promises that this nation was built upon. They were able to hope. But they became out of sight, out of mind. The chance for their children to go beyond a middle school education was wiped clean. Their ruthless days of working brought little to their families. The probability of being taken away from their children back to a place they no longer called home brought worry to their minds. They kept their hope and their family, so they decided to keep trying.

They refused to learn. Their children would try to teach them, but before they could speak, they became conformed into the systems. They became worried their children would accept a different way of life and possibly start accepting "those people." It was unacceptable. They passed laws and put up high fences to protect their own. These fences allowed only those who looked like them to come across and be welcomed. Slowly there came news of other walls in different countries being abused and broken by the people, so they built a bigger and better one. They put borders between their states, signs separating their cities, fences around their houses, and locks on their doors. "Finally," they thought, "a safe place." But they were wrong. Communities lost the ability to understand. The joy of individuality was pushed in the shadows, and the American Dream was created. Generations of them decided to forget. So they forgot.

@Dan *The U.S. has built about 650 miles of barriers and walls between itself and Mexico. Still under construction, more border wall is planned.*

Released

She flew into the office on a subdued weekday morning. She always possessed a good deal of energy, but today she was as wired as a blow dryer in the bathtub. Talking as fast as any decent superhero, she buzzed on and on and on. Slower! *Más despacio!* We laughed. She dug into a purse big enough to carry groceries, spare car parts, or a small child, and pulled out a letter. Crumpled and creased, it looked like the old love letters my mom had saved from my dad when he was stationed overseas in 1954. We got the hint: *READ THIS!* She handed us the letter and we knew within a few lines what was happening. The "blow dryer" bounced up and down from the current that flowed through her. We stood in the midst of the energy, looking at each other. *Seventeen years,* she said, she had been waiting for this letter for *seventeen years.* Nirvana was singing "Smells like Teen Spirit" and Ross Perot was running for President as she began the process of becoming officially visible. After seventeen years of paper after paper, form after form, interview after interview, payment upon payment, she received the sacred nine numbers that deemed her a legal, visible, official being. Soon, she said, as soon as she could, she would get herself on a plane and go to her mother. Her words flew into the electric atmosphere and fell with despairing reality back to the earth. She hadn't seen her mom in seventeen years. Of course not! She had been restricted. She had been contained. She had been held here. And time had moved on. She started a family. With no mother at her side, she had breathed by herself through every birth pain. No grandmother had held those babies at baptisms, birthdays, or graduations. The stories and wisdom that pass from mother to daughter had been fractured. Loss. Grief. Surrounded by such hope at this present moment. A visit, after all this time. A mother and daughter, separated from each other by a line in the sand, soon to be re-membered with each other. We didn't know whether we should shout with joy or anger.

Re-invented

She lay under the piece of artwork, cut red fabric, which became illuminated by the way the wind carried it up and down. The red grazed the soles of her feet when she raised them to the sky. Her head poked out of the cut holes, waiting patiently on her knees for the wind to take its turn and pull it up over her head. Her little sister called from the laundromat across the street to beckon her inside, away from the coming storm. The clouds bloomed as the wind picked up speed and bent the sound of her sister's yells away from her ears, leading to a response of "*Que?*" The people of the town rushed away to close down their homes, taping or stuffing towels in the holes or broken sections of the houses. She noticed the cool change in the breeze, the dry leaves that started to fall around her feet, and the silence that hummed with the washers and dryers across the street. Her connection to the land was much greater than most, she knew, simply because of the way she was taught. The land was not an object to be used; the land was a being. It breathed with every blade of grass that broke through the surface, and it choked with every dust storm. Her touch became gentler as she grew older. Her understanding of the give and take that it took to become one with the land became deeper. She would see her mother come home every day after working in the fields, with her long-sleeve shirts and sweaters on a ninety-five degree day, and listen. Her mother would tell her, "I thank the land every day for what it gives my family: food on the table and healthy babies at home." She remembered these exact words as she pressed her face to the earth. The tips of the grass skimmed her face like her father's mustache kisses. She breathed in a deep breath and opened her eyes to look across the street at her sister jumping up and down frantically, then jetting inside. The drops began to pour down, instantly soaking her clothes.

With one more deep breath of the new cool blend of grass and rain, she walks across the street and inside the laundromat. She stares out the window of her building and watches for the moment when the land takes a breath.

Re-birth

Piero della Francesco found her in 1467 and named her *Madonna del Parto:* You embraced my consciousness as your hand slid down your womb full of child. I painted. Your eyes endlessly stared at the floor in a knowing that you would never hold your head high. I saw. You were there alone in being, but in spirit you were guided. I imagined. Your blue dress parted in the middle; a birth that would never cry out, breathe, or make a whisper of a sound. I realized. Jorie Graham encountered her once more in the late 1900s in her words of "San Sepolcro": "In this blue light I can take you there, snow having made me a world of bone seen through toYou caught my eye at the museum on the day I held a notepad in my mind. You peered into the depths of me without ever taking a glance in my direction. You looked sad that day, eyes curved down, a disappointment? No...a sorrow. The crowds crowded in disrespecting swarms, seeing but not noticing your private presence: you, tragic, forever stillborn. You and I both want a need of revision. You stained my mind as I walked home past the sun-warmed lemon trees. You were re-envisioned through my words.

I recalled her once more in your image: You told me you were pregnant. Your five-month-old growing womb became unveiled as your sweater was parted. You were restricted of movement, carrying a child, a secret. Your eyes positioned themselves downward in worry and shame. You heard my voice in loving tones and acceptance, but you did not see me past your doubt. You stayed as I left, but I would never leave you for long. You pushed me away as I pulled closer. You shut me out of your world. You pushed me down past my own knowledge. You blamed me. You hurt me. But I still love you.

Re-vision

You told me you had to go. You said that you had a vision and that you had to follow it. And, as is the case with most visions, the particulars were vague. The gravitational force that pulled you into this dream was such that no human effort could resist. Like the prophets before you who were called into the unknown, you would go alone. I fell in love with you even more. Plans were made, and days flew by. You said you were ready. You said you were nervous. You said you would come home as soon as you could. "Remember your toothbrush!" I said. Time to go. I would take you to the airport. Only one question remained unanswered: "How would you return?" They asked to see our passports. You handed yours to me, and I handed ours to them. They looked at you for too long. They told us to pull over. They escorted you inside. They told me to wait. You told me it would be okay. You told me you loved me. You said that you would be right back. You were wrong. I asked and looked and begged and pleaded for you. The response came as harsh as a stone upon stone, sealing the tomb: Northwest Detention Center. Three days later, you walked from your cell into another cell and I could see you through the glass. We picked up the phones that

@Dan *Immigrant detention is big business. Private prison companies played a major role in writing and passing Arizona's racist "papers please" law.*

led to nowhere. Your entire being had changed. Your journey, my love, was just beginning. Our journey, my love, was just beginning.

Re-encounter

This is the beginning, to discover emotions and feelings and somehow put them into words, not only in my mind, but on paper. I have laughed and cried about this for days, but still cannot seem to rummage through the words of my vocabulary to find that one word I need to move on, not forget, but remember. These English classes have not seemed to take me anywhere, nor have they opened my eyes to some new miraculous way of writing that makes the audience's hearts wrench. But here it goes.

Re-told

The day he dies is going to be unbearable; a word even worse than that. I still haven't heard all the stories; maybe my next visit will consume me in his every breath. I know it will. I'm not ready for him to go, I never will be. Every time I sit at the piano, every train that streams by, every pumpkin will remind me of him. I will tell my children about him, so often they will love him as much as I.

Regret

I walked around the buildings, grumbling. Doors always left open, this time the garage. *Errgh!* Can't they ever remember? Maybe it was just a random mistake. I closed the door tightly and left. The next day, her calico eyes looked at me from the railing on the fence. Pretty, I thought, as I put the truck in drive. Days later, I caught a glimpse of her again, still staring at me. Strange. I opened the tightly closed door from nearly a week ago, looking for some misplaced tool. They were wrapped loosely together, their small bodies cold and breathless. Her babies. Oh God! What have I done?

Redeemed

We stood in the middle of the field. Sky the color of evening, hills the shade of a long days work. The knife split open the first melon of the year. Sweetness kissed our lips and dripped from our worn out hands to the welcoming earth. The fruit remembered the day its being first touched earth and felt sunlight. We laughed and ate.

Why?

Because we are the stories and visions. We remember and re-act. We are released, re-invented and re-birthed. We revision, retell, and regret. We are them and they are us.

With hope that one day we will be.

●

● Jill and Katherine's conversation partner was Dan Millis. He read Jill and Katherine's essay and sent the tweets you see in the margins. Find Dan's essay, "Frontera," on page 88.

Notes

[1]James Weldon Johnson, "Lift Every Voice and Sing," available at http://en.wikipedia.org/wiki/Lift_Every_Voice_and_Sing.

Questions \for Discussion and \Contemplation

1 What will the "slow example" of your lifetime be?

2 Why do you think it might be important to be aware of, and remember, the history of our world, the Church, or our country that has brought us to where we are?

3 What do you hope—against all odds—that the world, that your life, will one day be?

Conclusion
(or, "Now What?")

In the fall of 2009, Julie Richardson Brown e-mailed me and asked, "When can I call you? I have a question for you." When the conversation turned to: "Brandon and Christian think we would be good co-editors for this book," I was flattered, panicked, intrigued, uncertain, interested, anxious, and excited. That means *yes*.

And on a cold and rainy Friday morning, sitting on the floor of her office, we looked at each other, laughed nervously, and said, "So. Now what?" Then we realized just *how* exciting this could be. That first conversation, and the countless others—rapid-fire all-hours e-mails, short and long phone calls, "just a thought" text messages, and Facebook chats—are only the smallest glimpse into the great (both in quantity and quality) conversation that *It's Not All About You* has been.

But after all the conversations that got us here, and the one great overheard conversation that this book was designed to be, there is still no way to "tie a bow" on it and say: "Here are the things that we learned." There is no "three points and a prayer" for a sermon outline on social justice and witness. Maybe that is what you were hoping for.

Our hope from the beginning was that people would *talk*: to us, to each other, and to anyone who would listen. In a day when talk is constant, but listening is rare, *conversation* is a currency of real value. It is an exchange of ideas and ideals, of hopes and dreams, of fears and excitement, of misunderstanding and reconciliation. Conversation moves us forward, and moves us out: out of our own heads and into the world. Conversation takes on a life of its own and tells us, loud and clear: "It's not all about you."

This conversation has shown us that *the church is doing a good thing*. Churches of every size and stripe have members and participants of every ability and interest. And when church does church right, those abilities and interests find their way into the world and stand as *living* testament to the *written* testament. When church does church right, children who are raised in faithful surroundings become young adults challenged and inspired to live out their faith in ways that are real, meaningful, personal, vital, and life giving. When church does church right, the good news gospel of Jesus Christ is proclaimed mightily throughout the world, and, to paraphrase Francis of Assisi: "When necessary, we used words."

This conversation has also shown us that *the church isn't the only place good things happen* (and sometimes the church gets it wrong). Not easy to hear—that's why we saved it for near the end of the book! Many of the incredible young adults we know have incredibly painful stories of life in the church— which have led them to life outside the church. Sometimes the church is more of a closed community than an open one, where focus on its own survival blurs the vision of the reality beyond the door. Sometimes youthful hope and passion ignite and a dream catches fire, only to be dampened by the cold water of church bureaucracy—policies and procedures for approval (and disapproval)—finally squelched in: "That's not how we do it." Sometimes it's not just the radical idea but the entire person who finds his or her spirit called to stand outside the norm, and sometimes the church says, "That's fine. But you'll be outside of us as well."

Clearly the church is doing something right. Young men and women are choosing to spend their time in church, at church activities, wearing and saying and singing church things. And when these young men and women serve in local mission projects, spend a week on a summer mission trip, or even a weekend helping in the church nursery, they discover the gifts they have been given, and they are inspired to lives of service, offering those gifts back into the world. They learn to be faithful adults, to own instead of borrow their faith, and to live in a way that proclaims the faith they profess.

The church's biggest challenge, then, is to realize—and accept—that *it isn't all about the church.* The world will always roil with the cycle of creation, sin, judgment, redemption, and reconciliation. But the world may not always know those are the words for it. And maybe this book's conversation suggests it doesn't need to. When need arises—for food, shelter, education, health, safety, justice, equality, honor—need must be met. Maybe the church can learn that the meeting of the need is paramount, and the who-gets-there-first-and-how (and under what condition, and with what expected return) is secondary.

On that cold and rainy Friday morning in Julie's office, we said we wanted this book to be different. We wanted this conversation to be organic and meaningful, to rise out of real life and not be bound by the strictures and structures of policy and politics—or even the framework of "writing a book." We recognized that "justice" looked different in every context and to every observer, and wanted to highlight the multitude of ways that the "greater good" is lifted up, and the upended is set right. We hoped that young adults would be willing to tell their stories—honestly, unfettered, in their own words, and with their own emphasis. We prayed that we could move ourselves out of the way and simply let them talk: set the conversation free and enjoy the vast privilege and honor of overhearing the result.

I hope we have done that. I hope you have enjoyed reading, that you are inspired to serve, and that you will encourage action and activism and witness in those around you. Our hope was to strike a match to conversational kindling and let it generate its own heat and light from there. We hope it has.

And, if not, maybe it just means the conversation needs to continue.

So. Now what?

Courtney Richards

Contributors

KATHERINE BELL truly believes her ancestors of before have gifted her with words to tell not only her story, but theirs of the past and those who she will eventually know. She has the love of Rebecca, the compassion of Belinda, and the awareness of David. It's the sweetness of life that brings us together. Sweet tea. That's Katherine: just normal, but with a little bit something different.

JOSHUA DOBBS is a veteran of Operation Iraqi Freedom, newly married, a triathlete, and is currently the Clinical Manager of Non-Invasive Cardiology at IU Health's Methodist Hospital in Indianapolis.

JILL DELANEY lives her life in and around White Swan, Washington. Her days include coordinating the Learning and Serving program at the Yakama Mission, teaching speech/communication to local college students, growing organic vegetables for the RicoOrganics Cooperative, dreaming of opening her own coffee shop, and, best of all, hanging out with her best friend/husband, David Lemus, and their brilliant "children"—Junior, Rita, Che, Pepino, and Tecolote—as well as all of their wonderful friends and family.

KENDRA DUNBAR is originally from Columbia, Maryland, and is now living in New York City where she works for the General Board of Global Ministries of the United Methodist Church. As Executive Secretary for Youth and Young Adults, Kendra works with global youth and young adult networks linking young people from churches within the Wesleyan tradition with ecumenical and grassroots partners to provide opportunities for global mission education, capacity building, exchange, and advocacy. The aim of her work is to create space and opportunity for the development of young church and community leaders. Kendra received her BA in history from

Williams College and earned her MDiv from Union Theological Seminary. Currently she serves on the U.S. Trustees of the World Student Christian Federation and is also on the Board of Directors of the National Black Methodist for Church Renewal.

JENNIFER FISCHER, an educator and filmmaker, is the co-founder of the Santa Clarita Valley Film Festival and Think Ten Media Group/Generation Arts. Her work includes: "Songs of Palestine," a documentary short presented in conjunction with her Masters Thesis at Harvard University (writer/director/editor/producer); the award-winning *Rachel's Fortune* (writer/editor/producer); *The Hiding* (co-producer/editor), now available at retail and rental outlets; and the recently released *In Focus* (co-producer/editor). Jennifer received her BA from Sarah Lawrence College (2000) and an MA in Middle Eastern Studies from Harvard University (2003), where she focused on visual media and its role in the Israeli-Palestinian conflict.

JOE GEOGHEGAN is a student at American University in Washington, D.C., where he studies International Relations as it pertains to Peace and Conflict Resolution and International Education, with a focus in Latin America. As a news junkie, Joe spends a great deal of his time overwhelmed at the cruelty present in so much of humanity, but, at the same time, is more amazed at the sacrifices that so many people make to fight that cruelty and inequality.

CHLOE GRAMMER is a student at Bellarmine University in Louisville, Kentucky, where she is a nursing major and a member of the women's soccer team. She enjoys listening to all kinds of music, reading good books, singing in the shower, taking walks on fall days, and getting to the beach as often as she can.

MARC ISTOOK is a guy who wears a bunch of different hats in his life: church camp counselor, broadcast journalist, son, brother, Texan, California resident, amateur photographer, Trivial Pursuit aficionado, wannabe chef, TCU fan, and Disciple of Christ. None of these hats qualifies him to write this essay, but apparently bribing Courtney Richards and Julie Richardson Brown does.

AMY JONASON is a graduate student in sociology, studying subjects that are found at the intersection of religion, social movements, and urban life. When she isn't buried in reading or a DIY project at home, she enjoys song-leading at her church, sitting with friends around the dinner table, and being outside.

DAN MILLIS, born and raised in Arizona, has worked on border issues since 2005. He is the Borderlands Campaign Organizer for Arizona's Grand Canyon Chapter of the Sierra Club. Dan is also a volunteer with the border humanitarian aid group No More Deaths, and is the recipient of the 2010 Derechos Humanos Corazón de Justicia Award for environmental work. When not working or volunteering, Dan is probably mountain biking, rock climbing, or playing his old-school Nintendo.

JOSHUA E. PERRY teaches law and ethics at Indiana University's Kelley School of Business in Bloomington, Indiana. Previously he was on faculty at Vanderbilt University's Center for Biomedical Ethics and Society, where he worked as a hospital ethicist and taught bioethics and professional responsibility in the schools of medicine and law. Prior to life in academia, he practiced law as a civil litigator. He's married to Shelli Yoder, and they have three children—Ivy, Eden, and Oakley. If he's not in the classroom teaching or in his office researching/writing, Josh can usually be found outside hiking, camping, biking, or otherwise playing with his family and having as much fun as possible. He's also a bit of a politics and pop culture junkie. You can follow Josh on Twitter @jedperry or connect with him on Facebook at /joshua.e.perry.

COURTNEY RICHARDS is the Minister for Congregational Growth at Geist Christian Church in Indianapolis, Indiana. A graduate of Angelo State University and Brite Divinity School at TCU, she is currently a member of the Disciples' Week of Compassion Advisory Committee and previously a Disciples' representative to the National Council of Churches Ecumenical Young Adult Ministry Team. When not being about her ministry (and sometimes when she is), you can find Courtney either on a dance floor, following her musician pals, being Auntie Rev to her friends' kids, in the top row of a movie theater, or curled up with a book—and maybe some chocolate.

JULIE RICHARDSON BROWN serves as Team Minister for Youth Ministry for the Christian Church in Indiana and as Community Integration Coordinator for Family Scholar House, based in Louisville, Kentucky. She is also a founding member of nPartnership, an organization dedicated to best practices in youth ministry. She is a lover of fine coffee, dark chocolate, and good music. Her favorite author is Madeleine L' Engle; her favorite band is Indigo Girls; her favorite movie is *The Breakfast Club*. She is fortunate to have spent the majority of her professional career working with people who want to change the world. The authors of this book are no exception.

ERIKA ROMAN SAINT-PIERRE has been writing since she was young and wrote her first novel at age 10. She is co-author of the book *Locked In,* and president of Culturatti Ink, a publishing house focused on promoting culture and diversity. Her recent book, *Hoppa's Big Move,* is the first in her collection of children's books on cultural and social diversity.

NANCY SMITH-MATHER, a graduate of Furman University (BA, religion and sociology), spent several months in South America serving street populations in El Alto, Bolivia, then taught middle school at a charter school for refugee and immigrant students in Georgia. While completing a Master of Divinity at Emory University's Candler School of Theology, she coordinated a refugee ministry for families resettled in the Atlanta area. During the last two years, Nancy worked with the Presbyterian Church (USA), facilitating community development in Kenya and the Sudan in partnership with Church World Service.

SHELVIS SMITH-MATHER is an emerging scholar and practical theologian whose passion for social justice and reconciliation drive his work in the United States and East Africa. While pursuing two graduate degrees at Emory University's Candler School of Theology, he worked extensively to address issues of racial and socio-economic inequity. Shelvis is currently living in Kenya and directing theological initiatives for the Fellowship of Christian Councils and Churches in the Great Lakes and Horn of Africa (FECCLAHA). Through FECCLAHA, he works in partnership with the National Councils of Churches of nine countries as they engage in the region's political, gender, ethnic, religious, and land conflicts.

MICHAEL WAGNER offers *"Salamat"* ("greetings") from Juba, Southern Sudan, where he is seconded to a local Sudanese FBO (faith-based organization) though the Church of the Brethren Global Mission Partnerships Program. Michael's work consists of designing and implementing post-conflict, community rehabilitation and development programs in rural communities affected by the ravages of war.

KRISTEN WALLING serves as a Community Health Volunteer with Peace Corps Madagascar. She grew up in Shaker Heights, Ohio, and is an active member in the Christian Church (Disciples of Christ). She graduated from American University in Washington, D.C., with a degree in International Peace and Conflict Resolution, and plans to pursue a career in global health. She loves burritos and tells absolutely fabulous jokes.